Pull
Yourself *OUT*

of the

MUD

**Know and Love Who You Are
and Get MORE Out of Life!**

Tamara Johnson

New York

Pull Yourself OUT
of the MUD

by Tamara Johnson
© 2008 Tamara Johnson. All rights reserved.

Library of Congress Catalog Number: 2007940791

ISBN: 978-1-60037-375-6 (Paperback)
ISBN: 978-1-60037-376-3 (Hard Cover)

Published by:

MORGAN · JAMES
THE ENTREPRENEURIAL PUBLISHER ™
www.morganjamespublishing.com
Part of the MegaBook Series

Morgan James Publishing, LLC
1225 Franklin Ave. Ste 325
Garden City, NY 11530-1693
Toll Free 800-485-4943
www.MorganJamesPublishing.com

Logo Design by:
Lindsay Zelazny

Author Photo by:
Paul Gregory

**Cover & Interior
Layout & Design by:**
Bonnie Bushman
bbushman@bresnan.net

To Julia and Tatjana:

The strongest, most beautiful and capable girls I know.

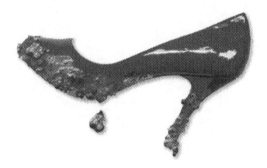

ACKNOWLEDGMENTS

This book began many years before it came to its present form. My first gratitude is to God for providing the experiences that make up the stories that fill this book, for blessing me with the insight to see the lesson in each experience, and for continuously moving me in the direction of completing this work. Without Him, I am nothing.

My sincerest appreciation also belongs to my dear Grandma Mower. She was my most vocal cheerleader and she worked her own magic to make my dream a reality. Thank you, grandma. I love you. To Grandma Ridge – you taught me about the essence of love. I'll never forget you for that. Thank you. Mom, you showed me what love and forgiveness are all about. You have been tireless in your efforts to teach and love me, no matter what we have been through. You have given me something that keeps me from giving up when love seems to be too tired to move! Thank you for your heart.

I have also shared my journey with many friends, mentors, and clients. Each of them has touched my life in unique ways that have contributed meaningfully to this work. Jan Hackleman, MFT and Dr. Pamela Henderson both mentored me with compassion and patience as I learned how to teach the healing process to my clients. I thank both of you for your tolerance of my stubbornly independent spirit and for working with me while I developed my therapist self. Dr. William C. Shearer and Dr. John Kohut, I thank both of you for believing in what I can do and cheering me on along the way.

So many of my women friends have shared their enthusiasm for the vision of this book. I am grateful to each of you for that support. Rachel Lazarus-Soto, thank you for helping me refine my definition of beauty. Pat-e Figueroa for your continuous strength and sense of humor, no matter the circumstances. Diana for your courage to never quit. All of my women friends and clients to whom I talked about this book while it was still just an idea, it was your encouragement that made me believe that I should complete it – your desire to read what I have to say. Thank you.

I am also deeply indebted to the women who have shared their lives and their concerns with me in my office at The Center for Healthy Relationships. It is always a sacred honor to be entrusted with the concerns, thoughts, hopes and dreams of my women clients – each one of you is completely amazing and beautiful. It is through your trust that I have been able to sharpen my vision of what it takes for the healing process to move forward.

Thanks to Laura Wiley, my editor; David Hancock, my publisher and Rick Frishman, who introduced me to David.

To Tatjana and Julia – you are the most beautiful gifts any mother could ask for. I am so sorry for the hurts that were part of your lives before we met. Know that with constant love and by never giving up, you and we can overcome any challenge. I love you, my dear daughters.

Finally, to the two most amazing men in my life. Dad, you have been my most consistent, nurturing, patient and informative mentor. You have been a strength in my life and my hope is that my "thoughts about life" can make you proud. Michael, my beloved, you have been here through so much of my growth process. Your patience and love during the creative process of this book and the creative process that is my life have been transformative. I look forward to many, many years of growth and service with you. Thank you for calling me beautiful.

WHAT WOMEN ARE SAYING ABOUT
PULL YOURSELF
OUT OF THE MUD

Well . . . there is nothing else to say but Brilliant!!! You have ultimately captured what all of us women need to know and then remember. It is about time someone wrote something for us women who are working on being good to ourselves and giving ourselves permission to do so. I think I had better come in and do some more work with you. I may have progressed far with your guidance but I now see I have so much farther go. Thank you for writing this book, Tamara. I know of so many individuals I need to give it to already. Most likely, I shall be buying the first ten copies.

— D.N. College Professor

Pull Yourself Out of the Mud had me laughing and crying. Tamara's affect on my life has been monumental. If she can get through my cynical, crusty, old hide . . . . she surely will start a revolution! What amazes me about Tamara is that she has such an impact on everyone who meets her, without even trying. Truly, Tamara walks the walk! She has single-handedly renewed my faith in humankind. I now believe it is possible for someone to talk the talk, walk the walk, AND not be a boring, bland person to be around! There is life within spirituality!

— Pat-e Figueroa, Manicurist

Pull Yourself Out of the Mud is a comfortable, familiar read. I recognized many of my own struggles as a woman through Tamara's examples from stories in her own life. Her proactive invitation to respond to what I learned about myself inspires me to return to this book again and again for counsel and to check my progress. This book brings hope for all women who wish to overcome those struggles that are uniquely ours as women.

— *Alison Cuyler, High School Teacher*

My life is so wonderful today because of the tools Tamara gave me. Thank you, thank you, Tamara for helping to make a happy and healthy mom for my boys.

— *Shelby, wife to Tom & Mother of three*

Pull Yourself Out of the Mud is a wonderful and heartfelt book. Since I have been working through it and seeking the personal guidance of this wonderful woman, Tamara Johnson, my life has much improved. I am starting to get my power back and I am looking forward to a better life. I have discovered that I have continued to do the same things over again and again. But now I am getting back on track. Not only is Tamara a warm and caring therapist, her concern for me makes me feel that she is truly my friend. Thank you, Tamara. You are a blessing.

— *T. P., Homemaker & Beloved Aunt*

Pull Yourself Out of the Mud a wonderful book to reach core issues for women who are on the path of empowering themselves.

I love the format and the questions in each chapter. As a Life Coach I would certainly recommend this as reading material for my clients! Bravo and Well Done!

— *Michelle Berard, Life Coach/Massage Therapist*

I have enjoyed the *Pull Yourself Out of the Mud* immensely and felt very empowered to achieve *any* of my dreams after reading it!

— *Brandie Davis, Real Estate Agent*

When my husband and I first started working with Tamara, I didn't know what to expect. All I knew was that our relationship was in serious trouble. Over the last couple of months, it seems that things have become a lot clearer. While working with Tamara, she invited me to read *Pull Yourself Out of the Mud*, and I began to understand past experiences and relationships differently. I've actually learned a lot about myself. I'm starting to understand why I interact with not only my husband, but everyone around me, the way I do. I'm definitely a work in progress. I have a long way to go with myself and my relationship. But being able to understand how I learned to be the way I am is helping me to understand how to change the negative view I have of myself into a positive one — in order to become the person I want to be.

— *H. K., Hair Stylist*

CONTENTS

INTRODUCTION:
WHERE MY JOURNEY BEGAN

It is 3:45am. My beautiful, strong daughter is sitting next to me on the floor, eating cinnamon toast. I sit here and contemplate how to begin the book that chronicles my climb to another reality of fullness in living. It is a journey I write about without knowing the outcome. And yet I trust the outcome to take me to a summit higher than before. I ask my daughter for permission to write about riding a bull. Her eyes sparkle! She comes out with an emphatic "Yes!" and her smile is contagious. And I know how to begin . . . .

I suppose the journey toward being more fully alive for women, really does begin with the dreams in our little girl's hearts. I am speaking of the little girl who serves as the inspiration for the first chapter of my first book, and of all little girls we teach, nurture and influence with the spirit we carry with us wherever we are on life's journey. It doesn't matter if that little girl is our own offspring or if she is a little girl we encounter in a chance meeting for a single moment at the grocery store. If we influence them, they are our daughters. And our influence can affect a daughter whose name we never learn, just in the way we hold our shoulders when we walk past her. This influence comes from our shared knowledge of what it is to be a woman. For my daughters, what it is to be a woman is communicated in my own fullness of being; from my developing self to theirs.

I am also speaking of the little girl's heart inside of each woman. The heart that knows truth. The heart that knows how to play. The heart that knows how to love deeply and without fear. The heart that we may have lost contact with during the course of "growing up." This book is about truth. It is truth that we may have lost contact with, but which exists, waiting for an opportunity to blossom, nonetheless.

It is about truth that each woman can possess for herself. And, in the possession of that truth, she bequeaths to her daughters a priceless gift: the ability to know truth and to allow that truth to lead to richness in living.

This book is about the legacy we each leave to our children as we provide examples to them of what living fully and joyfully looks like. But it is also about exploring our own dreams and noticing that we have dropped some along the way. When you notice one of your dreams lying dormant on the ground where you left it, will you pick it up off the ground and re-explore it?

I invite you to read this book with your heart open to the truths you may have ignored in your own life. If you are a woman who has dreams that you have not yet achieved, this book is for you. It is possible and completely within your reach to live a happy, fulfilled life no matter what your current circumstances. I invite you to take this journey with me into the exploration and re-kindling of your hopes and dreams. I honor you for all that you are. I ask you to discover the best in yourself. I invite you to begin your journey today. If you have already begun your journey of discovering your best self, congratulations! This book will help you continue in your process of awakening to the possibilities that you have the unique opportunity to develop. Take my hand, let's go!

In **Chapter One** I invite you to explore the assumptions you hold about what is achievable in your life. Beginning with Chapter One, and at the end of each of the following chapters, I have provided a section called "So, What Are You Going to do About It?" Here I invite you to complete assignments that will assist you to evaluate the topic explored in the chapter on a more personal level. Each assignment builds upon the last and supports individual growth and exploration. My goal is to inspire you to challenge long-held assumptions that have been limiting factors in your life. For example, the first assignment invites you to explore the following question: "What are your childhood dreams?" The invitation is to remember dreams you may have abandoned long ago. The first step in reclaiming dreams is to remember them.

Chapter Two explores the concept of childhood dreams more deeply. My childhood dreams included being a prima ballerina and finding true, fairy-tale love. As a child, my sister actually tasted her "world-class gourmet" chocolate cakes that she crafted from mud puddles. I am sure you had dreams, too. This chapter asks several questions, including the following: How did taking on grown up responsibilities become defined as letting go of childhood dreams such as these? Does growing up really mean we have to let go of those things that inspire us so that we can conform to generally held beliefs about adulthood that serve to limit our potential as women? This chapter explores how socialization, beginning as early as toddler hood, teaches girls to be "nice" and "polite" and "good," often at the cost of losing awareness of their own needs. In this chapter, we will explore how socialization has led to harmful effects for women in terms of encouraging us to accept culturally defined standards of beauty and social roles, rather than encouraging each of us to find our own truths. Chapter Two introduces the idea of emancipation as a process of growing into ourselves and embracing our individual needs, dreams and goals. Then, these ideas are applied to our understanding of how we interact in our most important relationships.

Chapter Three describes "muddy thinking patterns" that we adopt as habits and how those patterns introduce limitations. Understanding and changing these patterns cause us to feel better about ourselves and to deal more effectively in our relationships. For example, at the age of six, my child looked me straight in the eye and said: "You know. You are not the best mom in the world." Ah, the wisdom of a child! I use this example to illustrate how to avoid the tendency to disconnect bits of "wisdom" like this from the "bigger picture." In reality, my daughter imparted her wisdom while we were sitting on the floor, nose-to-nose, and I was flossing her teeth! When I responded to her comment by saying: "You are right! But, I'm the only mom you have!" she threw her arms around me and told me that she loved me. Would you have taken a comment like this from your child to mean that you are a failure as a mother? This example and many others in Chapter Three provide concrete ideas for preventing muddy thinking patterns from ruining your day, inspiring negative beliefs about yourself and wreaking havoc in your relationships.

Chapter Four explores the concept that significant people in your life may encourage you to maintain habits that are self-negating because when you keep yourself on the back burner, you make life more comfortable for everyone around you — at your own expense. This chapter offers the challenge for you to be completely honest with yourself about your own behaviors in order to recognize your motivation to put yourself down to keep others around you happy – even if it makes you *un*happy. Guilt, shame and the effects of childhood sexual abuse on adult relationship behaviors are also examined so that if you have been hurt by abuse you can begin to see how to break patterns of abuse that were imprinted to your heart during your early years.

Chapter Five begins with a humorous story about how I threw myself into the water at Lake Mead without a life jacket to save a set of $2 toys. The lessons in this chapter include taking personal responsibility for personal safety and well-being. This chapter also addresses the need for avoiding self-sacrifice for a cause that is less important than your own life, well-being or personal safety. When we care about other people, we must carefully balance between how much help we have the strength to give, we must evaluate how much of our help is actually helpful, and we must keep one eye constant on our own mental, emotional and physical reserves. Developing a list of self-nurturing behaviors, which many women do not have, is the assignment at the end of this chapter.

Chapter Six compares the emerging of feelings into our conscious awareness to the moving of soils in a garden. I once watched an educational clip that was part of children's television programming which featured a series of time-elapsed photos that began with a photograph of rich soil. Through the course of the next several photos, the soil remained unchanged as the sun was shown going up and down to represent the passing of several days. As the days passed, the photos showed the soil beginning to move, ever so slightly, over a single point in the photo. Then, the soil moved aside as the very tip of a sprout broke through. The plant began to grow, and the remaining photos showed the completion of the process until the plant was mature and produced a flower, opening toward the sun. Our feelings are often like the plant in those time elapsed pictures. The problem is that some women are in the habit of placing a box over the sprouting plant (their feelings) because the feelings seem too difficult to deal with directly. The feelings never see the light of day. Chapter Six provides education about this process and concrete steps for coming to understand that our feelings are our allies. They teach us about what is needed to develop and maintain healthy emotional, mental, physical and spiritual balance. This chapter also addresses the reality that women in domestic violence relationships close off their feelings as a means of survival. But if you are one of these women, this is the very strategy that will keep you stuck. You are encouraged to seek counseling or to contact the National Domestic Violence Hotline for additional assistance in escaping extreme situations in connection with what you learn from reading this book.

By the time you have worked through Chapter Six, you will have begun the process of de-constructing negative patterns in your life. In **Chapter Seven** I offer you the invitation to begin exploring your definition of yourself without the negative contributions of your old beliefs. This is specifically addressed in relationship to the reality that you may have abandoned the process of developing a personal identity when you entered your marriage relationship. Chapter Seven explores the affects of neglecting your personal identity in service to the joint identity of marriage and provides direction for making course corrections. Here, I implore you to give yourself Absolute Permission to be whatever it is that constricted rules have prevented you from becoming. In my case, it was "not okay" to be beautiful *and* to be loved. So, I sabotaged my relationship with a loving husband who had nicknamed me "Beautiful." My efforts at sabotage ended the day I realized what I had been doing and how my "internal rules" were being broken. For a few days, I walked around saying: "I give myself *absolute permission* to be beautiful!" It did the trick for me and works for many women whom I have helped to overcome contradictory internalized rules.

Chapter Eight explores the powerful transformation that happens when you develop the courage to really believe in your dreams. If you hold to them and do not let go nor give up when times become difficult, your dreams will materialize. This chapter explores obstacles introduced by time constraints, the passage of time, and others' negativity. In this chapter, I poke fun at the nay sayers and call them the SS (Skepticism Society). I outline the first three articles of the SS Constitution and point out that the very presence of the SS indicates that your goals are audacious enough and that you are on the road to successfully achieving your dreams, so long as you refuse to give up!

Chapter Nine challenges you to set your goals high and to recognize that taking risks and making sacrifices are essential parts of overcoming the obstacles to your dreams. This chapter also illustrates that fear is an invitation to faith. It outlines how to use fear to keep the growth process alive. I use a funny story about a Chihuahua to point out that the fear of something that stops us from moving forward is usually worse than the feared object, itself.

Finally, **Chapter Ten** is my personal invitation for you to think about the legacy you wish to leave to those who follow in your path. I invite you to begin the process of supporting and nurturing yourself in a community of supportive women, rather than participating in competition with other women. The challenge is to stop "going it alone" and join a world-wide network of support wherein women support and help each other as we build our dreams together.

To get the best use from this book, I suggest you begin with Chapter One and work through each chapter in succession. My strong recommendation is that you take the time to complete each exercise at the end of each chapter before moving on to reading the next chapter. The chapters follow a logical progression that is similar to the progression of growth I lead women through in my private practice. If you are willing to put in the effort, you can make positive changes in your life and relationships – no matter how fulfilling your life and relationships may be right now.

After you have finished this book and you find you want to take your learning to the next level, you will have several options. If you want to connect with other women who are interested in getting more from their lives and providing mutual support, visit my Worldwide Women's Support website: www.GetOutoftheMud.com. There you will find: free articles about developing your potential as a woman; my internet radio program that explores women's issues, relationships and self-growth; and information about additional training opportunities that I offer in the form of half or full-day seminars and weekend Women's Growth Retreats. Begin the journey today and I will provide you with the tools necessary to develop your potential as far as you wish to take it!

CHAPTER 1

I CAN RIDE A BULL!

Think About It:
Do You Really Want To Diminish Her Dreams?

My youngest child is a delightful, funny, active, very strong willed little girl. About six months before I began writing this book, she was watching a rodeo on television with great interest. So much interest that when I called her for dinner, she refused to turn her eyes from the scene she witnessed. It was as though she were in a trance. In a breathless voice, she simply said: "Wait!"

She watched, barely breathing, as a rodeo cowboy carefully lowered himself down to a seated position atop an angry bull. The bull, corralled into a small space that forced him to remain still enough to be mounted against his will, was required to submit only so long as the iron gate leading to the open arena was closed. But, as soon as the gate latch was kicked open, the bull raged in fury as it bucked, twisted, kicked and fought until the cowboy was thrown, as a rag doll, to the ground. When that cowboy was thrown off, my child still refused to come to dinner. She watched again, with increasing interest, as each man who attempted to conquer the bull was mercilessly thrust to the ground.

I stood, watching; pulled in by the same scene that mesmerized my daughter. In my mind, I was wondering what a man would have to be thinking to do such a thing. I watched as arms were twisted beyond their natural positions and body parts were nearly crushed. Once thrust to the ground, panic ensued as the man was removed from the ground before he was crushed by the furious bull. It was a life-or-death struggle, yet these men rode angry bulls for sport. Surely, they knew that each time they mounted the bull, the episode would end in defeat! Yet they continued. I stood clueless about what drew them to the sport. Yet, like my daughter, what I saw in each cowboy's efforts enthralled me. Then I was shocked out of my absorption in musing about the fitness of mind of a bull rider by my daughter's proclamation: "I can do that! And I can stay on! I won't fall off!"

Next, I have visions of my 7-year-old child, a fixed expression of determination on her face, as she mounts an angry bull with the same kind of do-or-die expression as I see in her eyes at this moment, proclaiming victory over a bull she has never encountered, except in her imagination. The next picture in my head is of her broken body, since I know (in my "adult wisdom") that her 58-pound frame would be instantaneously evaporated in a contest with a 2000-pound angry monster-of-a-bull. That image is much more than I can bear, so I dismiss her statement of victory over bull riding and say something to her about how much she would get hurt. With that casual statement, I hope to distract her from the bull riding. After all, it is my job to teach my child about what is possible and what isn't – isn't it?

But . . . my child does not forget! For days, she talks about riding a bull. She goes to school and tells her friends: "I can ride a bull!" She comes home and says the same thing. She is oblivious to the realities of physics and social sanctions. In my desire to protect her, I am oblivious to her truth. When she watched the rodeo, she felt strong, courageous, confident, invincible. When I watched, I felt confused, afraid and incredulous. With her attitude, my child could, doubtless, mount any real or imagined "bull" she encountered in her life fearlessly and with confidence. My fears and concerns for her safety would teach her caution and trepidation. In her vision of bull riding, my daughter is taking her free, strong spirit on a journey that makes everything possible. In my concern about physics and social appropriateness, I stunt the growth of her imagination. However, I'm the parent, right? I know better because of my knowledge and experience. It is my job to "teach" her about what is safe, correct and reasonable. This is a defining moment and I define a reality that strengthens my child against danger. Right?

But will my unenthusiastic response to her proclaimed victory over bulls lead to the "I can'ts" she will grapple with in her future?

Do I want to be responsible for that?

Do I want to be responsible for teaching my child to see limitations instead of seeing possibilities?

So, What Are You Going To Do About It?

— That is the question I was asked by my mentor, who was encouraging me to see the metaphors in my own life. At the end of one of our conversations, I told him I did not get anything out of what had been said. His response was: "What are you going to do about it?" His question suggested that if I was to find meaning in our discussions, it was my responsibility to allow myself to be fully engaged in them. I needed to allow our conversations into my heart. I needed to allow them to challenge me. I needed to take courage to make changes in my life. With this question, he challenged me to take personal responsibility for the direction of my life. And so, at the end of each chapter, I include a section that asks the same question of you, the reader.

This is not simply a book full of nice stories of how I pulled myself out of the mud. It is meant to be inspirational; to encourage you to reach for more in your life and relationships. My challenge to you is that you do the assignments you find in this book and continue to bring yourself back to the same question: "What am I going to do about it?"

Assignment:

What are your childhood dreams? Have you ever imagined that you might change the world in some unique way? What did you dream of that you later decided was an impractical or impossible dream because others told you that you might get hurt? I challenge you to take some time to remember. Remember right now!

Then, get some paper and a set of crayons and draw your dream. Or take out your journal and describe your dream. Or, gather several magazines and cut out pictures to create a collage of your dreams. Whatever you do, do SOMETHING that provides you with a visual reminder of what you imagine. Make it tangible.

CHAPTER 2

THE BEGINNING, BUT NOT
TRULY THE BEGINNING

Start By Remembering Your Own Dreams

And so, I am oblivious to my little girl's dream of conquering the bull. Instead, my focus is on the practical, sensible, day-to-day duties of "real life." I am mired in the details of what we should have for dinner, when I will get the laundry done, how much homework my kids need to do today, and whether I will get to work on time. I do not have time for dreams that distract me from the practicalities of surviving on a daily basis. And what, in my blank-minded pursuit of the mundane, am I training my two daughters to do? I am training them to forget about their dreams in the service of the daily struggle to finish each day's activities and to never look beyond the present moment. When do I begin to teach them that life is about more than daily drudgery? How will they learn to dream, if I tell them that dreaming is dangerous?

These questions about their dreams bring me to wonder about where mine went. I think that if I had absolute permission to dream wildly, it would be that much easier for me to allow my children to do the same. So, I ask myself: What were my childhood dreams? When did I stop believing in them? Once upon a time, I believed that my dolls were really alive. They knew me. They understood the words I said to them. They interacted with me, albeit silently. And I was *the best* mother in the world! I took the time to love, to nurture, to play. My childhood dreams also included me as a prima ballerina. I believed I had the grace and talent to be the *most famous* ballerina in the universe! I went to see the Nutcracker Suite with my family and knew it was my destiny to be Clara. I saw Camelot in a live theater production and dreamed of my Sir Lancelot. All of these things were in my future. I knew my life could follow the feelings of peace, confidence and love I felt as "the best mother in the world," the feelings of grace, beauty and talent I felt as a "prima ballerina," and the love, joy and companionship I felt imagining my life as Gwenevere. In spite of my childhood dreams, I eventually learned the "realities:" that prima ballerinas aren't 6-feet tall, that Camelot is just a land someone made up, and that I would face the heartache of infertility. Did realities like these cause me to stop dreaming? Does it have to happen that way? Couldn't I have held on to those dreams and still pursued them tenaciously? Maybe I could have been the first 6-foot tall prima ballerina. Maybe Camelot could have been created in my own life. Maybe infertility blocked my path to biological parenthood, but I needn't stop my dreams of being a mother. I think part of the problem is in the definition of which dreams are realistic and which ones are not. My question is: who gets to decide which of my dreams are realistic and which ones are not?

I remember watching my little sister playing outside in the mud. Although it was not obvious to the casual observer, the cakes she made were not of dirt and water. According to her, their flavor was German chocolate. No one else would taste her cake to believe it. She tasted it. And her conclusion was that she was a *world-class* chef! She must have felt so competent and creative. Nothing that anyone else said could convince her that mud was not gourmet chocolate! Could the imposing of a "realistic attitude" toward the cake squelch the dreams of an aspiring chef? I watch as my little girl plays with her beanie babies. They talk to her and she talks to them. Her imagination flourishes. Who am I to tell her that her beanies are not real? What does she feel while she imagines this way? Who am I to change the possibilities that exist in the thoughts and feelings of her imagination? Is it not imagination that provides the creativity and the fuel of dreams?

So I ponder the question of where my childhood dreams went and what gives me "the right" to extinguish my child's dreams. As I try to answer that question, the answer seems to exist in the reality that somewhere in the process of growing up, we forget ourselves. We forget our dreams. I think we forget because we accept the training of adults who have themselves forgotten how to dream. I think we come to accept a definition of the words "grown up" to mean that we forget about all of our childhood passions and wildly imagined dreams in the service of "responsibility." And we come to the belief that responsibility is mutually exclusive with play, big dreams, enjoyment, relaxation and/or self-care.

Think of it. Do you know anyone who has the means to be able to play hard? Do you respond by saying: "Good for them!"? Or, does the flattening of your own dreams lead you to believe that someone who has "made it" enough to be able to afford the luxuries of a vacation home or regular outings to resort spas or enough time to really play can do so because they were given their parents' money, they somehow cheated, or they were lucky? It is difficult to imagine transforming a wildly imagined dream into tangible reality—so difficult, that we often believe it can't happen, even for other people. But ask any of these people, and they will likely say that they worked really hard and never gave up on dreams simply because day to day realities sometimes provided obstacles to those dreams.

I think it is time for a new definition of "grown-up responsibility." I think we need to see it as taking charge of the actuality that the realization of our dreams is doable, simply a matter of believing and following through. Yes, we must take care of the daily details of sustaining life, but simply focusing on the details of sustaining life is what I call "survival mode." And living in survival mode *is not* the same as taking grown-up responsibility. Growing up and taking on adult responsibility includes finding a way to make playing and striving for our dreams and nurturing ourselves a regular part of our daily activities. In order to do that, we need to understand what gets in the way of thriving. I believe the best way to understand what happens that stunts our thriving is to explore the developmental process that we call growing up.

WHAT GETS IN THE WAY

How Being A "Good Girl" Squashes Your Dreams
& How To Take Your Dreams Back

Growing up is an interesting and precarious undertaking. When we are born, we cannot tell the difference between our self and our caretakers. Being fed, being changed, and being held, are all events that we assume (with whatever ability of assumption we have at this early stage of development) occur because we *will* them to happen. Our awareness, at this time, is in the present moment. We become aware of a need because of the discomfort it causes; and we respond to the discomfort by loudly protesting the condition of discomfort; we cry. If we are lucky, a nurturing caretaker quickly satisfies our need. If this happens routinely, we associate simply having a need with having that need met. Our response to having an unfulfilled need becomes the catalyst that sets our caregivers into motion, as though our needs control their behaviors. As infants, we are self-centered and focused on pleasure and the avoidance of discomfort. Nothing else.

By the time we reach the ripe old age of toddlerhood, we begin to recognize that there is a difference between our self and others. This is when we learn perhaps the most important words in the English language if we are to embrace ourselves as separate, autonomous individuals. The first word is "NO!" Other words of premium importance that we learn to use at this age are: "It is mine!" and "I do it!" Saying these words provides us with a sense of personal power and agency that we intuitively know is essential to our well-being. We understand that our survival ultimately depends upon our being able to direct our own behaviors, and we are willing and anxious to develop the independence that would eventually lead to complete emancipation from our caretakers. Then (as a product of our parents' well-intentioned desires to nurture us and help us grow), we were dutifully taught that it was not okay for us to use these tools of our emerging independence and sense of separateness;

of personhood. Instead, we (especially girls) were taught to "Be nice." Instead of being allowed to assert ourselves by saying "No," we were taught to take other's needs into consideration. When we said "It is mine" we were taught that we had to share. When we asserted ourselves by saying "I do it!" We were told, "Let me help you."

"Yes," you say, "but we must teach our children to be polite. We must teach them to share. We must teach them that it is not OK to say 'No!' because it is disrespectful." On these points I agree, but only to the extent that the principles of politeness and social grace teach socially appropriate behavior without sacrificing a girl's sense of self. At what point do we dismiss conventional wisdom about being polite, and teach our female children to honor themselves? At what point do we decide that when our child says "No" it is not rude, but rather a wonderful assertion of her own needs that deserves VALIDATION?! Is it possible, that from our early training, we began learning the process of making our own needs secondary to those of others?

In contrast, consider the training of little boys, who are encouraged to play competitively and aggressively. The toughest, most aggressive boy "wins." He does not ask for what he needs; he takes it and is praised for being strong and "all boy"! Perhaps, that is the beginning of where boys learn to balance their own needs with the needs of others. At some point, they learn that if they are too aggressive, other boys will not play with them. Consequently, they learn to balance their own needs with their need to get along with others. They already come to relationships knowing how to assert their own needs, but learn to soften their demands in order to maintain a relationship. It appears that boys begin their training early for being able to "hold onto themselves" within the context of a relationship.

By pointing to some of the differences in training between girls and boys, I am not suggesting that we encourage girls to play in the same way as boys do. I am, however, suggesting that because of differences in early training, girls and women are required to address the developmental task of attaining personhood as an ongoing process which requires balance between the pressure to be "nice" or "polite" and the requirement to care for their own needs as people. I believe that we can do this by encouraging our little girls to listen to and to honor their own experiences. An example comes from my daughter who can ride bulls without falling off.

I met her the week before my 30th birthday. I had traveled to Yugoslavia a year prior to meeting her and had gone home with empty arms and a broken heart—a failed adoption attempt. But a phone call a year later invited me back to the hope of becoming a mother and a dream that had seen me through heartache and disappointment after disappointment for seven years. On July 5, 1996, I was escorted to the "toddler room" in the orphanage, and my new daughter was introduced to me with the words "There she is." All of the other children were together in a room designated for children of their age. My child was walking up and down the halls, the orphanage worker's finger tightly gripped in her fist. With just a few teeth in the front, she grinned as she commanded the attention of the worker through her persistence. She was fair skinned, all chubby and dimply, and she had a dollop of blonde ringlets on the top of her head. When I held her in my arms, the orphanage workers warned me not to form the idea that this was a "hold me" baby. They were right. I was to learn that she was independent, strong willed and happiest to be on the go!

However, I witnessed the shackling of her brilliant, independent spirit when the orphanage worker invited me to feed her lunch. The worker handed me a spoon and a small bowl with bits of potatoes and ground beef in a slightly thickened broth-like liquid. Then, the worker tied a large towel around my daughter's neck, and left the room. The amazing thing was that with the towel tied around her neck, it was as though my child forgot she had hands! My brand new daughter opened her mouth and leaned forward, in anticipation, just like a helpless baby bird. I patiently spooned the first mouthful of food to her. To my surprise, she immediately swallowed with a gulp and opened her mouth in a split-second, leaning forward for more, as if to tell me that she was starving for the next bite. I paused, a bit puzzled by her behavior, but did not change my pace of feeding. The next moment, the orphanage worker came to check on us and saw that I was feeding this little bird too slowly and took it upon herself to correct my feeding procedure.

The worker took the bowl from my hands and began to feed my child at such a speed that I was stunned. She rapidly shoveled each spoonful into my daughter's mouth at a speed that required the child to gulp each spoonful without chewing and re-open her mouth for the next within a half-second from the last. Suddenly, she was transformed from a hungry little bird into a garbage disposal! The pace was so fast that I was astounded that my new daughter could even breathe during the process! The entire bowl of food was gone in less than one minute! And there sat my new baby, uncomfortably full and belching the air that she had swallowed during her rapid-fire meal. The orphanage workers had found an efficient way to get as many children fed as quickly as possible, but this method was hardly beneficial to the children in the long run. Right there in that little room in the orphanage in Yugoslavia, I made my first parenting decision: to teach her to eat slowly.

Seem like an easy task? Well, it had some complications. First of all, she delighted in the independence she felt when she was no longer forced to keep her hands under a towel during meals. Feeding herself was a joy that she quickly claimed as her right. But she was not accustomed to chewing her food. So at each meal, I was required to place her in her high chair, place her food on her tray and watch her carefully. I encouraged her to take small bites, by regulating how much food was on her spoon and by monitoring the size of the pieces of food on her plate. This was a struggle because she wanted to manage the feeding on her own! The problem was that she did not chew! So I became remarkably adept at quickly unstrapping her from the high chair to hold her with her head toward the floor while I firmly patted her back to dislodge a strawberry or other piece of food from her windpipe. I spent hours sitting in front of her while she was eating, modeling chewing motions and saying "chew." I waited while she became angry with me for taking food away for the refusal to chew. Then, I gave it back so long as she mimicked my chewing motions. Finally, she learned to chew and was out of danger of choking, so I began to trust her with food.

But the training was not over simply because she no longer choked on food after learning how to chew. The next hurdle was to teach her when she was full and to stop eating at that point. She had been trained to eat until she was extremely uncomfortable. (Imagine how our country's problems with obesity would be exaggerated if each of us had been trained to eat as this child had!) So I began the habit of feeling her tummy with my hand and giving her something else to do when I thought her tummy felt full, but not distended. Interesting training that was! By the time she was six, my child would come to me, lift up her shirt for me to feel her tummy and ask: "Am I full, mommy?"

Yikes! So, when she came to me to ask that question, I began to tell her, "It is *your tummy*. It will tell *you* when you are full." It took a few years, but by the time she was ten years old, she could confidently tell a grown up who tried to tell her to "finish your plate" that "I am full, and when I am full, I stop eating." My daughter has learned to listen to her internal signals of hunger and satiety. She honors that. Sometimes, an adult will insist upon imposing the "finish your plate" rule so that no food is "wasted," even after my daughter states that she is full and stops eating. At those moments, she looks in my direction and says: "Mom! The rule is I stop when I am full, right?" I respond by telling the person who is concerned about how much she eats that "If she is full, she does not need to clean her plate." I want to honor her process of valuing her own experience. Her growth process illustrates a part of her development that began the moment I decided to teach her how to slow down when she eats. Can you imagine what her life would have been like if she could never tell when she was full? Or, if she looked to external cues to decide whether or not her meal had satisfied her hunger?

This story illustrates the basic point that from the time a child is born, until the end of her life, her most important task is a developmental process called emancipation. My daughter required sensitive and specialized training to emancipate herself from her orphanage feeding rituals. Emancipation is the process through which a girl or young woman learns to know who she is and to nurture and to embrace her authentic self, rather than valuing what others impose upon her about who she is and what she should do. When she accomplishes this, life becomes fuller and richer. She can be guided by her intuitive sense of what is good. Her goals and plans are achievable. She develops satisfying relationships. (The same is true for boys, however as I have stated before, boys are encouraged to embrace themselves much more directly and earlier than girls are; if girls are encouraged to emancipate themselves at all.) Let us look closer at the concept of emancipation.

The dictionary[1] defines "emancipation" as "freedom from political, moral, intellectual and social restraints offensive to reason or justice." A complementary definition comes from the world of family therapy and psychology[2]: "The normal separation of children from the parental family. Such emancipation is an evolutionary task in a nuclear family system and culture. The emancipation must occur physically and geographically, as well as psychologically and socially. The separation is the culmination of many forms of increasing psychosocial separateness between parent and child." During the course of participating in the personal growth of my clients, I have come to understand that emancipation also involves the process of coming to understand which of the emotional "truths" learned while growing up are invalid, based on their pragmatic value in the life of the emancipating individual.

That is, as we begin the growth process by examining our beliefs, we come to recognize that there were things we were taught as children that seem true to us, simply because of their familiarity. With deeper exploration, however, we find that there are objective truths (for example, the reality that children deserve to be loved and nurtured as they grow and develop) and emotional truths. Emotional truths are those things we learned that *feel* true, but that may or may not be objectively true. An example of an invalid emotional truth might be the belief that boys are stronger and smarter than girls. When we recognize that an emotional truth is invalid, usually because it causes negative attitudes and feelings about our self, we begin the process of letting go of the invalid emotional truth in order to develop more self-embracing, validating truths about our self. This process is emancipation.

Emancipation also implies that a woman recognizes and frees herself from constraints imposed by cultural systems of power. It implies that she resist the pressure to ignore what she knows about herself in order to embrace overarching "truths" about women that originate in cultural norms and rules. One of the most obvious examples of how women are pressured to accept "truths" which are not self-generated can be found in cultural standards of beauty. As generations have changed, standards of beauty have been defined by various examples of beautiful women. Specifically, standards of beauty with regard to weight have traditionally instituted tremendous pressure to conform, while the standards, themselves, have been rather arbitrary and unstable over time. The most striking example of the shift in weight standards accompanying women and beauty comes from the weight-to-height trends of the winners of the Miss America pageant[3].

As Figure 2-1 shows, all of the six women who reigned as America's most beautiful women in the 1920's were within a healthy weight range. In fact, the first four Miss Americas weighed

Figure 2-1

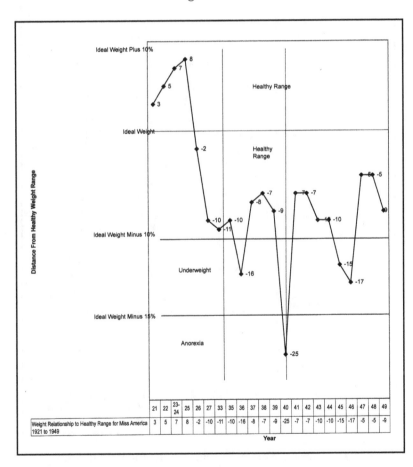

Miss America Weight Considerations for 1921 to 1949

in within the upper 10 percent of their ideal weight range[4]. However, the weight trends for Miss Americas in the subsequent decades show a sometimes dangerous downward pattern (See Figure 2-2 and Figure 2-3). Winners in the 1930's all fell within

Figure 2-2

	51	52	53	54	55	56	57	58	59	60	61	62	63	64	65	66	67	68	69
Weight Relationship to Healthy Range for Miss America 1951 to 1969	-8	-7	-12	-8	-16	-14	-5	-10	-11	-15	-14	-9	-10	-9	-6	-20	-14	-10	-10

Miss America Weight Considerations for 1951 to 1969

the lower ten percent of the healthy weight range, except one, who registered as underweight. The trend toward maintaining weight in the lower range of healthy continued in the 1940's, 1950's and 1960's. During each of these decades, most of the

Figure 2-3

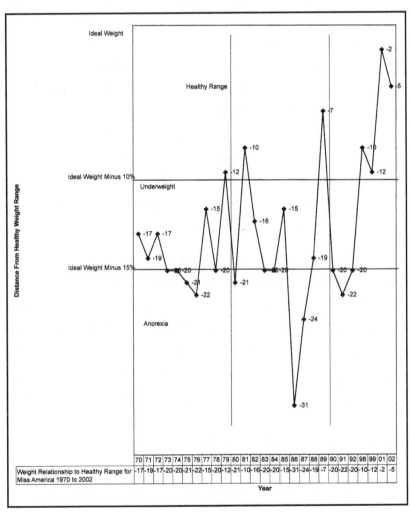

Miss America Weight Considerations for 1970 to 2002

winners weighed within the lower ten percent of healthy weight, with two women falling in the underweight category in the 1940's and the 1950's and four women registering as underweight in the 1960's. The downward weight trend continues and is much worse in the 1970's, 1980's and early 1990's. During that time, nearly all of the winners of the pageant fell into the underweight category. That is, they weighed over ten percent *less* than the expected ideal weight for their height. Only 3 winners during the years between 1970 and 1991 fell within the healthy range. And they weighed in the lower ten percent of the healthy range. An interesting note is that the diagnostic criteria established by the American Psychiatric Association for Anorexia Nervosa includes maintenance of weight fifteen percent below minimally normal weight for age and height. During the history of the Miss America pageant, the height and weight for seven winners qualifies them for the diagnosis of Anorexia Nervosa!

The pageant stopped publishing heights and weights for winners of the pageant from 1992 until 1998 and again after 2002. In evaluating a graphic display of the weight trends, one wonders if the pageant organizers decided to stop publishing heights and weights of contestants in an effort to stop the downward weight trend. It appears that the move to stop publishing those statistics had the effect of encouraging contestants to shift focus away from weight as a significant factor in criteria for Miss America, because the four winners between 1989 and 2002 again registered within the healthy range. It appears that when society focuses on weight as a criterion for beauty, the pressure for women to conform to unhealthy standards increases. And the pressure successfully influences women to conform. The mere fact that in the first years of the Miss America pageant, women who were in the upper end of the healthy range were judged as beautiful, yet as focus on pageant winning progressed, the winners became thinner and thinner illuminates the exaggerated focus on weight as a component of beauty.

An analysis of the weight trends of Miss America winners brings us to the question of who might really be influenced by this data. Some people speculate that the body image of young girls and young women is not influenced by such things as Miss America pageants. The interesting point is that when I was nine and ten years old, I watched that contest and cried with the winner as she was crowned. I watched the pageant with dreams swimming around in my head of being on that stage and competing with those beautiful women. However, when I was nine and ten years old, both of the women who won the contest fit the weight criteria to be diagnosed anorexic. How could that not have affected me? In reality, it did.

A striking and disturbing report has been recently made by BBC news in the UK regarding the desire of even younger girls to be thin[5]. The document, entitled Six Year Olds "Want To Be Thin," reported that according to a study at Flinders University of Southern Australia, over 80 girls between the ages of 5 and 8 were interviewed and, according to their article in the British Journal of Developmental Psychology, 47% of those young girls wanted to be thinner. My question is: Who is influencing these girls and girls like them all over the world? I would suggest that influences from the media and parental attitudes are teaching young girls to reject themselves while they are yet very young. And this should not come as a surprise. After all, how can a child whose mother rejects herself, based on these influences, escape the same self-rejecting patterns?

It is my belief that unrealistic role models presented to young girls who are just growing into their female forms place those girls in precariously vulnerable positions. They are set up to reject their own bodies because these do not correspond to the unrealistic ideals presented to them. Even in recent years, I have encountered young girls who begin the process of self-rejection when they begin to experience the changes inherent in puberty. One such change includes the depositing of fatty tissue around the hips. It involves the metamorphosis from a boyish body to a woman's body. So many images in the media idealize a female form that is so thin that it resembles the prepubescent boyish shape, that girls in this transition see their own development as ugly, fat and abnormal rather than natural, desirable and beautiful. It is often this beginning attitude toward their developing bodies that later supports the onset of eating disorders. Eating disorders are maintained by virtue of a self-perpetuating cycle. First, self-rejection inspires hyper-awareness of body image and the decision to begin strict dieting and/or extreme exercise, and then the body responds to extreme dieting practices by craving calorie-dense food in order to avoid starvation. Finally, the cycle begins again, when over-eating of calorie-dense foods causes self-criticism and self-rejection. Once this cycle sets in, poor body image has taken hold and developing a positive sense of personal beauty becomes all the more elusive.

With the introduction to our womanly forms during puberty so often characterized by unrealistic images from the media, it is no wonder that so many women never learn to accept their bodies and spend so much time, energy and money trying to change them, rather than seeing and valuing the beauty they possess. It is a pity that we do not possess and practice rituals that celebrate, for example, the deposit of fat on the hips and tummies of pubescent girls. If this were the case, we would grow to appreciate and accept ourselves as women. Then, from a level of self-acceptance, exercise would become something to do for fun, and good nutrition would become an issue of self-care. Without self-acceptance, women engage in dieting and exercise that feels like torture to them, but they continue because the elusive goal of having a prepubescent boy's shape brings the hope of self-acceptance. The problem is that self-acceptance does not magically appear to most women who have tortured themselves to whatever they believe their ideal beauty standard is. The key is to find beauty and self-acceptance and then live a healthy lifestyle as a matter of self-love. Only then can any changes we decide to make be done in the service of nurturing ourselves. Only then will the changes be gentle and permanent.

On the topic of emancipating ourselves from the media ideal of beauty, it puzzles me to believe that so many of us would swallow the idea that an ideal body shape or group of facial features even exists! How can there be an "ideal" when there is so much variability? Additionally, how can an "ideal" represent beauty when there is so much beauty outside of that narrowly defined ideal? Women we idolize on television and in movies represent a *significant minority* of beautiful women that exist within our culture! But because the media focuses on such a narrow definition of beauty, we believe it and do everything we can to wriggle ourselves into the forced ideal. One exception I have seen recently is the campaign by the *Dove* soap company. They provide support in the direction that beauty exists along a wide range of differences with their "every girl deserves to feel good about herself" campaign. Imagine how much more we will embrace ourselves when we realize that there exists beauty that transcends cultural prescriptions, and when a woman becomes self-possessed to the extent that she knows and values herself for her unique qualities and imperfections. How powerful we will be as women when our own definitions of beauty are reflected back to us every time we look in the mirror!

I came a long way toward expanding my personal definition of beauty when I spent several months learning to belly dance. During my studies of the dance, I attended several events showcasing various dancers. I learned there that when a woman shimmies, she is ever so much more beautiful if she has some fat that jiggles while she moves! And, if she exudes an attitude of complete self-acceptance while she shimmies her full-figured womanly form, she is a goddess! I remember watching in awe as a very large woman shimmied and jiggled in front of an audience that was communicating complete acceptance of her with unfettered enthusiasm at the first event I ever attended. Tears streamed down my face as I watched her, realizing that she was beautiful and that the problem with self-rejection I had was caused by the reality that I swallowed someone else's definition of beauty—a definition that did not have room for my individual characteristics. What held my attention as I watched this dancer was the confidence she radiated. She knew that she was beautiful and she danced with delight, almost flaunting her beauty to an audience unashamed of their enthusiasm for her. Her beauty came from within as much as it was publicly displayed in her well-practiced skill. It was such a life-changing perception for me to see women being applauded for their beauty no matter what their size or shape that I believe every woman should belly dance! The experience brought home the reality that my beauty does not change with the trends. I am unique. Once I acknowledge to myself the ways in which I am beautiful, even if they are not in keeping with the current trend, my beauty will radiate to everyone who sees me.

This concept is skillfully illustrated in the Dream Works movie, *Shrek*. In the movie, Shrek is an ogre commissioned by the selfish Lord Farquaad to rescue a princess on his behalf so that Farquaad can become the Ruler of Duloc. The king had banished all fairy tale characters to Shrek's swamp, and in exchange for rescuing the princess, Farquaad agrees to remove them from the swamp. Intent on renewing the privacy of his swamp, Shrek agrees to rescue the beautiful Princess Fiona from the tower where she is guarded by a dragon. Shrek successfully rescues the Princess Fiona, and on his journey with her back to the town of Duloc, the two fall in love. The complication that prevents Shrek and Fiona from expressing their love to each other, however, is Princess Fiona's secret: having been the victim of a curse at the time of her birth, she is destined to turn into an ogre at sunset each day. Shrek, having only seen the princess in her human form, feels too ashamed to reveal his feelings for her. Fiona, fearful that Shrek would be repulsed by her nighttime identity, keeps her feelings to herself. The spell placed upon the princess can only be broken by "true love's first kiss." But, both Shrek and Fiona are too self-conscious to reveal their feelings for the other. Before the couple has a chance to reveal their feelings to each other, time runs out for them with the impending marriage of Princess Fiona and Lord Farquaad. However, with the encouragement of the couple's friend, Donkey, Shrek decides to take the risk of proclaiming his love for the princess, even though the marriage ceremony has already commenced. Just moments before Farquaad kisses his new bride, Shrek interrupts the marriage ceremony to proclaim his love. Shrek's interruption comes just as the sun is setting, and so Fiona has the opportunity to allow him to see her as an ogre for the very first time. Shrek's response to the change in Fiona is a further proclamation of his love. Fiona then tells him that she loves him, too and they exchange love's first kiss. The next moment is the climax of the movie wherein Fiona takes on "love's true form." When the transformation is complete, she is still an ogre and states, "I was supposed to be beautiful." Shrek responds by saying, "You are beautiful." Fiona, unsure that she can believe what Shrek had just said asks: "Really?" Shrek replies: "Really, really." So, Fiona moves with Shrek back to the swamp and they live happily ever after.

While watching the love between the main characters unfold, we see that Shrek had fallen in love with Fiona based on who she was and on her acceptance of him, not because of her beauty. It would behoove each of us as women to recognize (as Princess Fiona did after Shrek proclaimed his love for her) that our value is not found in our physical beauty. We must find value in ourselves, and then our understanding of how beautiful we are will come *as a product of* understanding our value as women! Coming to recognize our value as women and rejecting the idea that our value comes via how well we conform to cultural standards of external beauty would represent a significant step in the emancipation process.

The idealized "standard of beauty" is only one example of how we, as women, allow sources outside of ourselves to define who we are. There are many more areas where we would be wise to ask ourselves some very searching questions. For example, who determined that women make better nurses and men make better doctors? Why are more boys aspiring to becoming dentists than girls? When did we come to believe that boys are good at math and girls cannot learn math as easily as boys? Who decided that a woman should earn less money than a man who has a compatible job and similar training? Who says trucks and sports cars are for boys (little or grown up) and not for girls? It is true that the organization of societal norms like these helps to shape our culture and provide structure with which to define personal roles. But the question is: Do we allow those roles to *limit* us by allowing them to prevent us from following our authentic interests and talents?

I learned first-hand that some of the characteristics traditionally ascribed to boys rather than girls are not true. In the beginning, however, I believed the myth that boys are smarter, stronger, more even-tempered and more logical than girls. That belief prevented me from excelling in math although I was an otherwise very bright student. In beginning algebra, as a freshman in high school, my first quarter grade was an "A." But each quarter, my math grade would fall one letter grade from the previous quarter. The second quarter, my grade dropped to a "B". By the third quarter my grade was a "C". And the struggle for the entire fourth quarter was to keep my grade at a "C" and not let it drop any further, which I was able to do, but not without considerable anxiety and effort. During my sophomore year, geometry was a bit easier, and my final grade was a "C" for the class without as much struggle. Next, my junior year in high school included an Algebra 2 class, which I approached with great fear, having remembered my struggle in Algebra 1. My first quarter grade in Algebra 2 was a "B." My second quarter grade was a "C." By the middle of the third quarter, it was clear that my grade was continuing to drop. I still vividly remember receiving a test graded with a "D" at the top of the page. Devastated and panicked, I approached my teacher, Mr. Turner, after class. I did not have to say anything; I simply stood in front of him with tears in my eyes. Mr. Turner was a very wise man. He seemed to understand more than I understood about myself at that moment in time. With a smile on his face, he told me that as long as I took good notes in class, turned in all of my homework, and tried my best on all of the exams, he would not give me a grade lower than a "B" in his class. With the absence of fear, and no longer being plagued by the idea that I could not handle math, I *earned* a "B" in the class. Mr. Turner recognized that I was smart enough to do math and he taught me a very valuable lesson. He began to challenge the myth that I held that "girls can not handle math." I went on, in my college career, to study calculus, earning a relatively effortless "A" in each math course I took. My experience in my junior year in high school gave me the confidence that I needed to know that I could tackle calculus and succeed. The idea that I, a girl, was not good at math was banished by a very insightful teacher.

Through the whole process, I gained some very valuable insights that I use every time I encounter a girl who is struggling with the same myth about not being good at math. In my counseling office, when I see that familiar anxiety regarding math failure (it happens quite often), I invite the child to write a math problem on the white-erase board similar to the problems she is struggling with at school. We look at the problem together and I ask: "What are you supposed to do with this?" The usual answer is that the assignment is to "solve for x" or "plot a line," but that she does not know how to do it, even though the process has been explained in class. Now, I ask the magic question: "What do you know?" Usually, although the answer to the problem or how to derive it is not immediately evident, there is *always* information about the problem that she *does* know! So that is how it starts, and how the problem is solved. I just keep asking: "What do you know?" Eventually, the girl realizes that she knows enough to figure out how to do a problem that seemed daunting at first.

The point to this story is that anyone can ask the question: "What do I know?" It applies to so much more than math! It might be an amazing experiment to try asking ourselves that question any time we come up against a "rule" that tells us we cannot do something by virtue of being female. Imagine what a powerful tool we have when we face an intimidating situation and instead of withdrawing, we take a deep breath and say, "Ok. What do I know?" At that moment in time, the only thing we might know is that we do not know how to proceed and that we are feeling intimidated or afraid. Asking the question "What do I know?" can ultimately lead us to some very surprising and satisfying answers if we have the courage just keep asking ourselves the question.

Let us explore another example of how we can limit ourselves because we are girls. How many choices do we make that are "practical" while ignoring other choices that would be just as useful, but which follow our true desire. How often do we chose white paint for the kitchen when we would really rather choose red? How much more fulfilled would our lives be if we honored our own tastes and preferences instead of deferring to others? Before I married, I purchased my first car: a "sensible" family sedan. I purchased the car thinking I would marry in my not-too-distant future and would need a family car for the family (read: children) that I hoped would come soon afterward. The irony is that I got married shortly after I bought that car, but no children were born as I had planned. In fact, by the time the car was replaced with a newer, more reliable car, fertility treatments had proven frustratingly fruitless, and no children had ever sat in the back seat of that car.

Years later, after I had adopted two children, my primary car no longer fit into the "sensible" or "family" categories. It was a two-seater convertible roadster! It broke the rules of the kind of car a mom drives. But who makes the rule that says I cannot or should not drive a Prowler? Should I have felt guilt because I drove a very personal car when I had a family? No! (Furthermore, when I drove my car, I always made a point to identify my car as a "girl's car" whenever it was admired by young girls). Should I have felt bad about having a car simply because it was fun and fit with my sense of style? No! Did my ownership of such a personal car mean I was selfish? Maybe. But, consider the possibility that there is a brand of selfishness that allows me to feel so fulfilled that I am better able to attend to the needs of the others in my life for whom I am responsible. Perhaps, when I can be selfish, I give myself permission to refill my reserves of energy and warmth and love in a way that ensures I have *more* to give to others. The extent to which I can honor myself in such a way is the extent to which I gain value as a woman. In the time that transpired between my "practical" car and my Prowler, I had learned much about my value as a woman. We need not all run out and purchase an exotic car to find our value. The car serves as a metaphor for valuing and honoring ourselves. The principle I am attempting to illustrate here is that when we habitually negate our own needs to the "back burner," everyone loses because we are at risk of becoming so "burnt out" that we can give to no one. I am simply suggesting that when we have the choice, we make the choice that serves our own emotional, mental, spiritual and physical well-being. For example, when we find ourselves choosing between a "practical" shower, because it is quick and efficient, or choosing a luxurious, relaxing bubble bath, we should ask ourselves which choice would provide the most "fill" for reserves that have been depleted. The same principle can be applied to our choice of whether to scarf down a leftover peanut butter and jam sandwich that one of the kids did not finish, calling that "lunch" or actually paying enough attention to our own nutritional needs to have a salad with lunch and to drink enough water.

When we begin exploring how the reserves from which we nurture others get refilled or ignored, more questions emerge, forcing us to explore the limits we place upon ourselves. We cannot begin to consider the possibility of paying more attention to personal needs without calling into question the demands – real or imagined - imposed upon us by others. For example, who says that women should place their needs second to the desires of their children, or their husbands, or their parents, or their church leaders, or their employers? With these questions, I am certainly *not* suggesting anarchy or hedonism! But, maybe I am suggesting personal rebellion against the internalized rules we create that limit us. We must begin to question whether the rules we accept actually represent our own values or the values *we think* others would prefer us to have. For example, do we resist telling our spouses what we need, thinking they do not care enough to listen or that they might not agree? Will our parents actually reject us if we make independent choices that they may not have selected for themselves? If we complete a church assignment in our own creative style, does that mean it will not be acceptable to the church leaders? If we live our life in a way that is consistent with our belief system, but different from what other members of our congregation would do, does that make us wrong? Do we really need to forfeit our vacation time at work just because "everybody else does"? To test these perceptions and answer these questions for ourselves, we must value ourselves. Let us value ourselves at least as much as we value the others in our lives. My suggestion is that when there are competing needs, we should at least *consult our own feelings and needs* before sacrificing ourselves to the point of exhaustion and depression.

One of my favorite ways to illustrate this point is to ask young mothers when they eat. Young mothers often eat after everyone else has eaten. Sometimes, that does not allow any time at all for mom to eat because as soon as the family has eaten, they are off and running to other activities. In her efforts to keep up and to make sure everyone is happy and attended to, mom leaves even her most basic nutritional needs unfulfilled. If you are not a young mother or a newly-wed, the question still applies. Eating is one of the most basic needs we have, yet we often let a myriad of other concerns get in the way of attending to this very basic self-care. Some may say: I do not have a problem with *not* eating; I have a problem with *eating too much!!* In response, I have the same question: When do you eat? Most likely, you eat as a result of not considering your own needs when confronted with a conflict between your needs and others' needs. Then, you eat as a way of dealing with that disappointment and frustration. Overeating, just as under eating, is very often a result of poor self-care when confronted with conflicting needs. To correct it, pay more attention to yourself. It works.

I provided counseling to one young mother who could not understand why she was feeling so tired and depressed. She had always wanted to be a mother and was happy to fulfill that role. She adored her children, but sometimes felt resentment toward them. She sought my assistance to help her understand why, when she had the life she desired, she was depressed. One of the first things we discovered was that she believed that in order to be a "good mother," she should sacrifice her own needs to provide for the happiness of her family. I asked her when she eats. She explained that she really did not have time to eat. Then, she described the schedule of feeding her one and four year old little girls and that it was a challenge to keep both children busy and happy throughout the day. Then, at the end of the day, she would serve an evening meal to her husband and children, while she was constantly getting up from her meal at the table to do things like clean spilled milk, get the salt, or pick up a dropped utensil. By the time her family was finished eating, she rarely had finished her meal. But, her husband was home, so he played with the children while she ate alone. I taught her to make sure she ate regularly throughout the day while sitting down. She learned that by teaching her children to wait for her to satisfy her need for nutrition, she was training her children to understand that mommy needs to eat and that it is okay for mommy to take care of mommy. By learning this, she taught her daughters by example and transmitted to them some very important lessons about the role of a woman within her family. It is training that will prevent her daughters from feeling the same resentment and depression that their mother suffered. Something amazing happened when this young mother realized that her habit of leaving herself last to the point that sometimes she went an entire day without eating a meal left her feeling tired, resentful and often sick. She began to understand that "good mother" and "mother whose needs are last to be fulfilled" are not synonymous! It was a victory when she came back to my office to report that she was sitting down to eat regular meals, even if it meant that her family had to wait for her. She was delighted to find how much more patient and loving she felt and how her resentments were resolved by simply attending to her own needs.

So, along with the need to resist definitions that are imposed upon us by others, emancipation also involves making sure we are not always the last one in line. To do that, we must be willing to confront our own beliefs about what others expect of us. That means that we have to confront within ourselves the fear that we will risk disapproval by others if they are not cooperative with our need to become more of a priority in our own lives. We must be courageous enough to face those possibilities and confront them, rather than numbing ourselves and doing nothing to value ourselves.

WHERE DID I LEARN NOT TO VALUE MYSELF?

Your Early Development

Erik Erikson was a developmental psychologist who believed that at each stage of development, humans are confronted with specific crises, which provide opportunities for normal growth through development. If these stages are successfully mastered, development progresses and the individual gains greater ability to live and cope in the world. If not, growth is stunted and many life situations will bring anxiety and the inability to function. I believe that by looking at development as it is explained by Erikson, we can find clues as to what happens to women that teaches them to view themselves as less valuable than those around them. Let us review Erikson's theory.

During the first year of life, Erikson suggests that the developmental crisis involves the struggle between basic trust and mistrust of the world. When caregivers respond to an infant's need for care, the baby develops a sense that the world is a safe place and that her needs will be satisfied. So, as I had discussed earlier, when the baby believes that her cry is the catalyst for action of the caregivers, she learns trust. She cries when she becomes hungry, she trusts that she will be able to get food when she needs it. If she cries and cries and is not responded to, she learns that her needs will not be attended to and that the world is not safe. If her needs are sometimes satisfied and sometimes left unsatisfied, she will also learn to distrust. According to Erikson, the satisfaction of basic needs in infancy sets the stage for patterns of trusting in oneself and the world around us, even through adulthood.

In the second year of development, the crisis is represented in the struggle for autonomy versus the experience of shame and doubt. So, when as toddlers we learned to say "No!" or "I do it!" or "Mine!" we were struggling for a sense of autonomy. That is, we needed to know, in order to develop more completely our personhood, that we were our own boss. It is around this time that toilet training usually takes place, when the will of the child to control her own body and the will of the parent who wants to end diapering experiences conflict. The toilet training experience is a direct and open struggle for autonomy. My daughter was 36 months old when I began trying to potty train her. I purchased a book and a baby doll that pees and spent an entire week playing "potty" with my child. She knew what we were doing and could take her peeing baby through all of the steps, including giving a reward of a sip of soda to her baby and taking one for herself with each successive successful step in the process. The only difference between my daughter and her baby was that my child would not potty in her chair! Finally, after I gave up on trying to potty train her, she decided on her own, about two weeks later, that she was going to use the toilet. It was after I had given up and she saw one of her friends using the "big girl" potty. After all of my best training attempts, I was the one trained: that my daughter would do what she wanted with her body when *she* was ready! My experience with my daughter is typical of what Erikson taught. Especially during the "terrible twos," children are seeking a sense that they are capable of making choices independent of parental wishes. Successful maneuvering of this stage brings a sense of confidence that our bodies and our choices are our own. If during this time parents become overly-concerned with socialization or safety enough to disallow freedom of movement and exploration of the world within the limits of safety and reason, the child develops a sense of shame and self-doubt. Imagine, for example, that during our potty training struggle, I responded to my daughter's continuous insistence on soiling her training pants by scolding her and calling her a "bad girl" simply because her developmental schedule did not fit my idea of what was convenient. What message would that have sent her? Had I handled the potty accidents by shaming her, I would have probably also been likely to treat other types of accidents as if they were character flaws. These types of responses would have taught her not to trust herself because accidents were evidence that she could not measure up to others' expectations of her. Repeated experiences in opposition to her practice of autonomy would lead to doubts in her ability to make decisions and feeling badly about herself, even into adulthood. It would lay the groundwork for her to become overly concerned about others' expectations of her throughout her life.

It should be mentioned here that childhood sexual abuse during this stage of life interferes significantly with the development involved in becoming an independent, confident person. It imposes a lasting sense of shame and guilt that can be overcome through competent and compassionate psychotherapy, but requires a great deal of exertion. The reason sexual abuse interferes so significantly is because it challenges the concept that "my body is my own" in a similar but more profound way as a shaming experience during potty training does. With sexual abuse, the child is prevented from saying "no" or from asserting her own boundaries concerning her body because a powerful adult teaches her, with threats and with actions, that she has no control over what someone else does to her body. In many cases, it takes a woman a long time to re-claim her body as her own and to learn the concept that she does not have to comply with the wishes others impose upon her. To be able to learn this, she must first overcome a great deal of shame, guilt and fear associated with the actions of a powerful, abusive person from her past that maintains an overwhelmingly potent presence in her current emotional memory. For adult survivors of childhood sexual abuse, extracting the perpetrator from current emotional experiences is an essential part of healing that can be accomplished within the context of personal psychotherapy.

At this point, it is necessary to identify the difference between shame and guilt. Guilt is a feeling that occurs when a person behaves outside of the boundaries she has accepted as guidelines of appropriate behavior. A person can feel guilt about a behavior without feeling bad about herself as a person. Guilt is an appropriate response, for example, when we believe in being honest, but have lied about something to our spouse or to a close friend. Guilt provides a clue that a person has made a mistake, but does not imply that the person who chose poorly *is* a mistake. Shame, on the other hand, is a sense of being wrong *as a person.* Childhood sexual abuse often produces a profound sense of shame. A person who feels shame is typically very careful to always act within the constraints of behavioral appropriateness, usually according to definitions imposed upon her by others, yet still believes she is wrong.

A very simple example that illustrates the difference between shame and guilt often occurs when we break a diet. Without experiencing shame, an extra snack is simply an extra snack and permitted occasionally. But, when shame is part of our system of how we treat ourselves, that extra snack comes to represent everything that is "wrong" with us. So, after we eat a fresh, soft, homemade cookie our co-worker brought to the office, we berate ourselves. It sounds something like this: "I can't believe I ate that. What is wrong with me? Why can't I do anything right? I'm such a loser!" Then, we feel so badly about ourselves that we eat three or four more cookies (of course, we don't let anyone see us eat them) to try to soothe ourselves out of the shame. But, does eating *more* cookies reduce shame and self-doubt? I didn't think so! The cookies may temporarily reduce the negative feelings associated with shame, since eating can sometimes create a temporary numbing of feelings. But the cookies actually serve to make feelings of shame worse because most of the time when we go on a "cookie binge," we have trouble thinking and feeling good things about ourselves after the cookies are gone. Once we learn to shame ourselves, we apply it to ourselves in any situation where we make a mistake. It is a hard habit to break because it was likely reinforced for us over and over during our childhood experience. If simple mistakes were unacceptable during childhood, we will have to work very hard to make them permissible when we are adults. With entrenched patterns from childhood, shame transforms a simple mistake made by a normal human being into a serious tragedy performed by an individual with deep flaws of character. The practice of shaming oneself can also lead to the belief that random unfortunate events that sometimes occur in life present some kind of punishment toward the person who regularly feels shame. Shame encourages us to believe that discouragements come to us as part of our "lot in life." Fortunately, it is possible to overcome the practice of shaming ourselves. It requires our focused energy toward changing our patterns of thinking. Plainly said, shame is a serious error of belief that can be unlearned, freeing you to lead a happy, shame-free life.

Let us look deeper into how shame becomes a habit for some of us. I believe that the seeds of allowing others to define the self are planted in the autonomy versus shame and doubt stage of development. If a woman allows others to define her rather than defining and valuing herself, perhaps her first lessons in this behavior occurred when she was a toddler and chastised or "protected" from exploring the world in typical toddler fashion. Perhaps, the woman who experiences self-doubt when she is confronted with the choice as to how she will assert herself in the face of conflict was discouraged from claiming herself early in life: she was punished for saying "No," for example. When I speak of conflict here, I am speaking of those moments in time when a woman is confronted with the choice of taking care of her own needs versus caring for the needs of others. It is permissible and desirable for a woman to *choose* to care for someone else and place her own needs secondary from time to time. However, the optimal word is choice, here. Problems occur when a woman feels compelled to help or when she feels incapable of saying "No," even though her better judgment indicates a different choice. However, self-doubt, shame or inappropriate guilt are often responsible for the negation of a woman's own needs in service of the needs of others. When a woman allows this doubt to overpower the innate drive to care for herself, the woman suffers. When a woman suffers in her ability to care for herself, those whom she cares for suffer, as well. I will speak more of this in Chapter Five.

Between ages of 3 and 5, Erik Erikson has identified the crisis of initiative versus guilt. This stage determines whether a woman is able to motivate herself toward self-initiated behavior or is bogged down by a sense of guilt that prevents her from pursuing her goals. Hesitancy to attend to self-care can be traced back to guilt resulting from failure in this stage of development because between the ages of three and five, girls are closely modeling their mothers' role-specific behaviors. That is, if a developing four-year-old sees that her mommy is exhausted and never takes time out for herself, to even sit down to eat a meal, the child develops an inherent, subtle belief that "mommies don't eat." Later, when the four-year-old has grown-up, initiating self-care in the form of securing adequate nutrition for herself after she becomes a mother will become a task that feels like unacceptable behavior.

During the school-age years, ages 6 to 12, the crisis has to do with feelings of industry (and a sense of accomplishment in completing school assignments competently) or feelings of inferiority when she compares her own work to the work of her peers. When a child fails to feel successful in this task, she grows up to continuously compare herself to her friends, neighbors and acquaintances. In her own mind, she never measures up, even if she appears to the outside world to be the quintessential wife, mother, homemaker or employee.

The next crisis identified by Erikson occurs in adolescence. It is a significant crisis which complicates the lives of many women in terms of their ability to provide self-care in the presence of conflicting needs. The crisis is between personal identity and role confusion. Role confusion is what happens when a woman does not differentiate between her personal identity and her role as wife, mother, employee, sister, friend, etc. Instead of seeing herself as an individual with unique qualities and abilities, she defines herself in terms of how well she accomplishes the tasks related to mothering her children, for example. Role confusion is often what is responsible for a woman's experience of "empty nest syndrome," because after a lifetime of devoting herself wholly to her children, she discovers that she has not developed any part of herself besides the part that is a mother. Her identity and her role became confused as one in the same. When woman has successfully negotiated the crisis of identity versus role confusion, she may be able to identify herself as a strong, intelligent, capable, free thinker and involve herself in activities that allow her to enjoy those parts of herself. She may recognize that she is creative and pursue her creativity through painting, writing, dance or other creative outlets. When the crisis is successfully negotiated, she can more easily identify and develop the unique qualities that are hers and which can bring joy and fullness of living to her life and to the lives of her loved ones. She is aware of and personally responsible for the development of interests and talents. She is courageous enough to know that developing those parts of herself that are uniquely hers will allow her to more effectively care for others in her charge, because developing herself fills the reserves from which she gives to others.

When a woman has not developed an independent sense of identity before marrying; her view of herself shifts from that of "daughter" to that of "wife." If, during her adolescent years, her pursuit has been toward finding someone to love her rather than developing a respect and love for herself, she begins her adult life in an other-directed fashion. She often goes from the mindset of wanting to please her parents, to wanting to please her spouse. The desire to please is not derogatory, per se. It is only negative in the sense that without a personal sense of identity, she will seek to please in a childlike manner, rather than as an adult, seeking reciprocity within the relationship. When a woman marries young or marries the sweetheart of her childhood, the crucial part of developing her identity that includes pleasing herself often gets lost. I thought it an interesting experience when I became engaged to my first husband. When the announcement of the engagement was made, my intended husband was given "Congratulations!" and I was told "Good Luck!" Perhaps, the people expressing their sentiments to us were subtly foretelling the demise of a mismatched relationship! That is impossible to tell, but I believe that congratulating the intended husband while telling the bride-to-be "good luck" carries the implication that he is increasing his value and that hers is the work of making the marriage successful. The tradition calls up the image of her bringing him his slippers and pipe at the end of his workday while she continues to cook and clean in order to please him. Please don't misunderstand; I am not suggesting that there is anything wrong with traditional role assignments in marriage, so long as the differences in traditional roles do not include a concomitant assumption that the woman's role relegates her to a position of lesser value. It should be recognized that partially as a result of social sanctions and socially prescribed roles, the marriage relationship can begin with an imbalance of power. And the woman who has not developed a sufficient sense of self will tend to subjugate her personal sense of identity to her role as wife; since the outcome of success or failure might fall, in her eyes, on how good a wife (housekeeper, lover, friend) and mother she can be. Her efforts become focused on pleasing her spouse, and she forgets herself. Then, when children join the union, she can quickly lose herself to the desires and needs of her children.

Occasionally, women clients of mine have described this process when attempting to tell their stories of development within the context of marriage. One client, Sarah[1], continuously passed the responsibility for her personal well being to her spouse. Married 20 years, Sarah's expectation for marriage was that if she was happy, she credited her husband for that happiness. If she was sad, she looked to him to solve the problem that caused the sadness. If she was angry or tired, these experiences were often her fault. Never during her experience of any emotions

---

1 *Not client's real name. Names and significant details given in these examples have been changed in order to protect confidentiality.*

did she ask herself the questions that characterized personal responsibility for her own emotional and mental health. If she was sad, she never responded to the sadness by asking herself: "What is this sadness telling me about myself? What do I need to do for myself so that I can feel soothed and able to experience feelings of sadness as they naturally occur in this situation?" Instead, her attitude implied: "I feel sad. Where is my husband? I need to tell him that I'm sad so he can make me laugh and this sadness will go away." Now, don't get me wrong! When I'm sad, I really enjoy having my husband hold me if I need to cry. But the difference between this example and crying in my husband's arms is the understanding that the sadness is *my responsibility* to experience and to work through. By crying in my husband's arms, I *am not* giving my sadness to him to repair. I am not a little girl any more, although it feels good to be held as if I were! And, it is okay to be held as if I were a little girl, so long as I understand that those little girl feelings belong to me and so long as I don't expect my husband to parent the child within me in order to make my hurt or sad feelings go away.

The point I am trying to make with this example and by splitting straws in terms of what a woman is doing inside of herself while being soothed by her partner is that when a woman loses herself in a relationship and passes the responsibility for her well-being to her partner, she is expecting to be re-parented within the context of an adult relationship; she seeks to meet his needs in a nurturing fashion and emotionally delegates her psychological well being to his care. This produces increased pressure on and increasing feelings of inadequacy for her spouse. He married an adult woman, and increasingly finds himself with a dependent and needy little girl. Hopelessness develops when he is unable to care for her emotional needs or heal her childhood wounds. She has merged herself into an enmeshment that does not allow her to see herself as an individual within the context of her relationship. In her eyes, they are one emotionally and his is the responsibility for her happiness or misery. This woman is, therefore, unaware that she can choose between completely submerging herself into the relationship and holding onto herself as an individual in her own right. If she is able to hold onto her individuality within the relationship, she can give to the relationship from a place of strength. And if she holds on to her individuality, she can receive support and comfort from her spouse during times of need without exhausting his emotional resources. If only she knew that developing a strong sense of self could lead her there.

When a woman leaves adolescence without having developed a sense of identity, her relationships also become fraught with a sense of isolation because the crisis of early adulthood is that of intimacy versus isolation. And true intimacy cannot be attained without a clear sense of personal identity. The enmeshed, completely submerged woman causes her spouse to feel smothered and suffocated because of her endless neediness and inability to sufficiently provide for her own emotional stability. So her relationships feel lonely because others withdraw from her in order to preserve their own sense of identity. In reaction to the isolation caused by others' withdrawal, women tend to attempt to overcome the isolation by becoming "doers." They begin to use their actions to try to bring others closer to them. Instead of being women who are able to enjoy their relationships and to be comfortable with simply being in and enjoying their relationships, these women are constantly trying to win connection with others through their actions. The specific action in question is not as important as the feelings connected with them. When we allow our anxiety about being connected to drive our actions, the actions make others uncomfortable, whether we are presenting someone with a birthday gift, cleaning a friend's home for her, or running an errand for our spouse. Neither should anxiety drive our efforts toward being attractive to our spouses. That should come from a sense of inner beauty, confidence and love—not fear. It is very important to examine our motivations and develop our actions based on principles of love and compassion, rather than on feelings of fear and anxiety.

In counseling, I have met women who are perplexed by their spouse's aloof nature. They complain that he is distant and does not seem to care when she cries to him about what she needs in their relationship. In truth, he is often feeling overwhelmed and at a loss to make his wife happy. (The belief that it is the husband's job to make his wife happy is a myth often shared within a relationship that involves the coupling of two role-confused individuals.) Feeling hurt and isolated, the woman does not ask herself "What am I doing that might be making my husband uncomfortable? How can I close the distance in our relationship?" Instead, she asks: "What is wrong with him? Why doesn't he care about my feelings?" She feels desperate to relive the warm, soothing feelings that existed in courtship. She believes it is his job to heal her emotions. He is overwhelmed. She responds to feelings of abandonment by yelling at him about leaving his dirty socks on the floor. Or, since she has a long-term habit of pleasing others, she assumes that he has abandoned her because she has not been enough of a "good girl" and will begin to seek validation by overachieving. She will work tirelessly to keep their home spotlessly clean. She will work out harder, thinking that losing weight will gain his affection. She will dress for him. She will try anything she thinks will please him enough to close the emotional distance. Most of the time, however, outside of her awareness is the reality that all of these routines to capture her husband's affections appear all the more needy to him and he feels more and more guilty about not being affectionate toward her. The result: more distance within the relationship. The solution is in the woman focusing on her own personal growth and emancipation process, so that she can become whole and self-sufficient enough to participate as an equal partner in her relationship. In the process, she is sure to learn that as an equal partner who can validate herself, she will garner respect within her relationship.

Many times, when I point out the need for personal development and emancipation to women, they have no idea how to accomplish the task. The emancipation process takes place when a woman begins to question "universal truths" which are placed upon her by others. As she questions the "universal truths" she will: 1) come to understand which foundational moral principles she will embrace, 2) choose not to abandon them as she becomes stronger in her personal moral belief system, 3) enhance her foundational knowledge of who she is and what she believes, and 4) develop a clear sense of self-defined identity. In order to understand how to initiate the emancipation process in her own life, each woman must first identify the rules set in place for her while she was growing up. Think of the rules imposed upon you. Sometimes, these rules are characterized as the "shoulds" we carry around with us. For example, "You should clean your plate because there are starving children in Africa." The problem with this rule is that it may be partially responsible for keeping us fat! The rule causes tension at that very moment when, in our attempt to be conscientious about stepping away from the table when we are full, we feel guilt about wasting food. By simply taking time to evaluate our experience at this very moment in time, we can find telltale signs that the "shoulds" are at work. By paying close attention to our feelings, we will usually find ourselves feeling that we will be "in trouble" if we break the rule of throwing away food. At this moment in time, if we ask ourselves "How old am I right now?" there may be two different answers. Chronologically, we may be forty years old, but inside we probably *feel* much younger. It is not unusual to feel like we are six or seven or even younger when we examine our feelings at the moment the "shoulds" pop up and start causing conflict between things we were taught during childhood and what actually works for us in the present time.

The reason this occurs is because, in our psyche, some things exist in time capsules as if they are frozen there from childhood experiences. The phrase "I feel like a kid again" refers to activities that bring positive reminiscence, such as when a memory is relived and enjoyed. Think of the last time the smell of a familiar childhood favorite food brought back vivid memories of your childhood home. This is a positive example of experiences stored in time capsules. Some of those frozen-in-time moments are made up of unpleasant memories, however. During our growing up years, whatever the circumstances were, our caregivers had patterns of behavior and specific rules that were imposed upon us over and over again. Some of their behaviors and rules were not good for us, but made things easy or more convenient for them. Examples of these rules and behaviors include insisting that children must be "seen and not heard", children must obey their parents without resistance upon their first request, or it is okay to hit, yell at, shame or otherwise abuse a child who is not adhering to the rules as desired. Especially when our caretaker imposed punishment that was harmful to our emotional well being, we developed a sense of guilt and fear associated with the rule that we broke that resulted in unreasonable punishment.

So, for example, if staying out past curfew resulted in sound beatings during adolescence, we would be hesitant and anxious about breaking curfew even years later, as an independent adult. This is true even if we did not break curfew, but witnessed dire consequences when our siblings did so. As an adult, we may not be consciously aware that we are "breaking curfew" and experiencing anxiety as a result; we simply feel a vague uneasiness that we do not really understand.

That anxiety will lead to compulsive behavior, which in this case may be leaving a dinner party at 10:00pm, although the festivities are scheduled to last until midnight. Imagine, for example that you are attending such a party with a date. If, suddenly you are so uncomfortable that you *must* go home to soothe the anxiety, but your date is not ready to leave, there arises a conflict of needs and more anxiety! In this case, rather than insisting that your need to go home be met, you would be better served to examine the compulsion. Ask yourself some questions.

Where does the compulsion to leave early come from? Is it your own grown up desire or an archaic rule from your childhood that no longer works? These are questions related to emancipation from childhood constrictions. When you recognize that the anxiety arises from the imposition of outdated childhood rules, you can then *choose* to abandon an outdated rule in the service of grownup choices. So, at the dinner party, once you realize where your anxiety is coming from, you can say something to yourself like: "It's okay for me to stay out late now. I'm not a child anymore. I won't get into trouble for this. I'm not doing anything wrong. It is okay for me to have fun and to decide for myself when to go home."

Most often, the rules imposed upon us were not directly stated. A child whose single mother is bedridden with depression learns to perform all of the daily duties of caring for herself, her mother, and younger children in the family. At the age of six, she already knows how to prepare food, bathe and diaper the baby and clean up after the family. Years later, she is depressed herself and cannot understand why she always feels compelled to provide care-giving to others, even complete strangers, who are quite capable of caring for themselves. Upon exploration, we discover that she has a long-held, subconscious fear that if she does not take care of someone who is not caring for themselves, she will die. It was a very true circumstance of her childhood. *Someone* needed to provide her and her siblings with food and other basic needs during childhood. She stepped up to the tasks and performed them because of her awareness that her behaviors were necessary for survival. Her task as an adult, however, is to recognize that although she experiences anxiety each time she thinks about or attempts to limit her contact with needy people, the anxiety is compelling, but not related to her present-day situation. As soon as she is able to recognize this and soothe herself by telling herself something like: "Nothing bad is going to happen to me if I do not help this person. She is capable of caring for herself and if I do not help her, she will find someone else who will," she will be free to make her own grown-up choices that have less to do with obeying childhood rules and more to do with following her own goals.

YOUR EMANCIPATION PROCESS BEGINS NOW

Figure Out Where You Are Right Now
& Where You Want To Be

There are some very good questions we can ask ourselves when we are working on our emancipation process. To get some idea of where you are in the process, ask yourself the following questions. Do my actions reflect what I believe and who I really am? Am I carrying around beliefs that were given to me by others, but that I do not ascribe to wholeheartedly? What is my belief system? Who would have me abandon my own beliefs in the service of their needs? Must I abandon my beliefs, needs and goals to make others happy or to gain others' love?

These questions illuminate the reality that each of us has rules that surface from our childhood that prevent us from growing and achieving our own goals and dreams. As we endeavor to uncover and correct these experiences in ourselves, we get better and better at recognizing subtle constrictions that keep us stuck in childhood modes of behaving. So, as I explain emancipation, it brings me back to my original question: when did I begin to believe my dreams were impossible? It happened a long time ago. Growing up, I was the friend that many of my peers sought out for counsel, advice and comfort. So began a dream of growing up and becoming a therapist. But I graduated from High School believing that I was not smart enough or strong enough to accomplish the goal of attaining a higher education because of emotional and medical struggles I wrestled with during my high school years. During those struggles, I developed beliefs about myself that made it easy for me to abandon my dream of becoming a therapist. Five years later, when I got married, my first husband saw my potential and challenged me to reach for my dreams. The dream came alive again. Today, I am a therapist. But as I have grown, my dreams have grown, as well. Years ago, at the beginning of my educational career on the path toward being a therapist, I was dreaming wildly and said that I was going to write a book for which I would be interviewed on television. Somewhere, during the course of my undergraduate and graduate educational experiences, surviving the crisis of infertility, adopting two children, opening a successful private practice, and pulling myself out of the mud of a loveless marriage, I lost the dream of becoming a nationally-recognized author and lecturer. I lost my grip on my dreams through those struggles, but today, I am not so quick to let my dreams fade away. I have realized that holding onto my dreams in order to see them become realities is just as much about hanging on during a dynamic learning process as it is about making a single decision to follow those dreams *no matter what*.

What follows chronicles my journey of re-claiming my dreams. My hope is that this roadmap will lead other women to their own dreams. Let us set out on this journey with a vision to change the patterns of how we interact with ourselves. Let us evaluate the limits we place on ourselves or allow others to place upon us. Let us grow beyond the limits of what we thought was possible!

So, What Are You Going To Do About It?

Did you do the last assignment? What did you remember of your dreams? Now, it is time to think about what gets in your way.

Assignment

Look at the project you created that represents your childhood dreams. When you look at it, do you experience thoughts like: "I could never really do that"? Write down all of the objections that come up for you when you think of obtaining your wildest dreams. What are the "shoulds" connected to you giving up your dreams? Where did they come from?

Think of whom in your life (past or present) would be most likely to discourage you from reaching for your dreams. What did they say (or what would they say) about what you are doing right now? When you actually obtain what you dream of, how will they respond?

Now, pay attention to your feelings when you think of this person. How young do you feel?

Write a letter (you will never send) to the person or people who contributed to the "shoulds" that influenced you to abandon your dreams. Recognize that you are no longer a child and can make your own decisions about the direction of your life. In your letter, remove permission from the person or people who discouraged you from reaching your dreams. Tell them that you give yourself permission to strive for and reach your dreams.

Now, read your letter to yourself and give <u>yourself</u> permission to go after what you dream of. You can do this for yourself every time you feel anxious enough about the pursuit of your dreams to quit. A little anxiety can be productive, but don't let the anxiety suffocate the joy in the journey toward your dreams.

CHAPTER 3

GETTING OUR FEET STUCK

Recognize & Change Negative Thinking Patterns

Several years ago, my children and I went on vacation to Lake Mead in Nevada with my family of origin. The vacation featured a houseboat that slept eight adults, a speedboat and two jet skis. At the cove we selected as our campsite, the children were excited about playing on the shore and we, as a family, would be able to enjoy each other's company, completely unbothered by any other vacationers. My children and I were riding in the speedboat as we approached the shore, and they wanted to get off the boat. I saw it as my responsibility, as their mother, to get off the boat before my children did so that I could help them through the shallow water to the beach. What followed was a painful experience that serves as the title metaphor for this book.

I jumped from the bough of the boat to what looked like solid ground under waist deep water. It was not solid. As soon as my feet hit the ground, they sank into thick, slushy mud. Hidden under the surface of the mud, there lay several sharp stones. I found myself stuck, knee deep in mud that was most surely more like quick sand than anything I had ever encountered. The sharp stones mixed into the mud hurt my feet. I attempted to pull one foot out of the mud, only to find that as I pulled one foot out, the other foot was driven deeper into the mud and stones. I was in pain, and I was stuck. I wanted nothing more than to get myself out of the mud, but with my own strength and the resources I had within me, I could not.

About eight feet away, I could see the anchor ropes that secured the houseboat to the shore. Eight feet may seem like a short distance, but the journey might as well have been a half-mile because each step in my struggle to move myself closer to the rope meant more painful experiences in stone-laden quicksand. Finally, I reached the rope. It was quite a relief to grab onto that rope and pull myself out of the mud. My only hope for pulling myself out of such a painful experience was in reaching for something higher than myself. Then, after finding the safest route to the beach, I instructed my daughters to grasp the rope as they got out of the boat, so that their exit toward the beach was not painful or difficult, as mine had been.

This painful experience of extracting myself from the mud on the shores of that lake is much like the process of emancipation. Participating in relationships with others and with ourselves in ways that require us to negate our own needs and, perhaps, to hurt ourselves is like feeling sharp rocks on our feet in quick sand. It hurts. When our feet are stuck in the mud, we are unable to create our own patterns of interaction based on reason and self-respect. The mud discourages us from experimenting with our actions because being stuck in the mud necessitates focus only on survival. We are not interested in thriving, but rather in coming out of it alive. So we react in automatic, unconscious ways that have historically worked to ensure our basic survival, but which prevent us from thinking and acting for ourselves in present time. We may find ourselves stuck in the mud due to the attitudes and behaviors of those around us and due to our fear of confronting those attitudes and behaviors within our own reactions. But, with certain age, the responsibility for remaining stuck in the mud or for getting ourselves out of the mud is ours alone.

One of the first ways that we begin to take responsibility for ourselves is by recognizing those thought patterns that keep us stuck in the mud. There are many "muddy" ways of thinking. When we accept these ways of thinking, our feelings are affected. For example, if we think we are competent, beautiful women, we are likely to feel good; to feel happy about ourselves. On the other hand, if we think we are incompetent and repulsive to look at, we will most surely be depressed and discouraged. What follows are some of the common ways that we as women sabotage ourselves with "muddy" thinking. I will describe several types of "muddy" thinking, in random order[1].

Disconnected conclusion — One of the ways we, as women, frequently sabotage ourselves is by drawing conclusions regarding our worth based on arbitrary, unfounded or unfavorable judgments. Sometimes, when we have made a mistake or when someone is critical of us, we allow that mistake or criticism to represent everything we know about ourselves. We draw a negative conclusion based on a disconnection from the "bigger picture." A very clear example of this comes to me from an interaction with my daughter when she was about six years old. I was sitting on the floor with her in the bathroom, flossing her teeth, as part of the morning routine before taking her to school.

She was sitting on a stool, and I was sitting on the floor; our noses could not have been more than eight inches from each other. In her "childlike wisdom," she looked at me and without blinking said, "You know. You are not the best mom in the world." No, it is not a typo! She said I was NOT the best mom in the world!

Now, I had several choices in terms of how to respond to her proclamation. Had I been stuck in a habit of making disconnected conclusions, I might have lost my head! I could have taken her declaration as the jumping off point to self-pity. If my child, at the age of 6, already knew that I was not the best mom in the world, I must be doing a terrible job! In fact, I could draw this arbitrary conclusion even further to the obvious and that I was, in fact, one of the worst moms in the world! If I already doubted my competency as a mother or believed that I did not show enough love, caring, nurturing, etc. toward my child, I could have taken her words to heart. I would have been beginning with a strong personal bias that my worth as her mother was questionable and from that point, drawing an unfair conclusion about myself and my worth as her mother. In fact, my conclusion would have been unfounded and disconnected from the reality that I am a pretty good mom. Further, the disconnected conclusion would have been made without any supporting evidence that I was actually the "worst mother in the world". Had I followed this line of reasoning, I could have found myself doing any number or things: crying hysterically, screaming at my child, eating a pound of cookies (you can fill in the blank with whatever you might have done!).

Fortunately for me and for my daughter, my thinking was not characterized by a habit of drawing disconnected conclusions. In the very moment that my daughter stated in her matter-of-fact wisdom that I was, in fact, not the best mother in the world, I smiled. The preponderance of evidence indicated that the very fact that my child felt confident enough to share her observation with me could mean that I am a pretty good mom because she felt safe enough with me to share her thoughts about my parenting. So, I did a quick, 30 second evaluation of the situation and responded to her like this: "You are right! But, I am the only mom you have!" With that, she gave me a hug, told me that she loved me, and was ready to go find her shoes.

There are other ways in which we can draw disconnected conclusions about ourselves as a way of harming ourselves. We can have one "bad hair day" and conclude that we are the ugliest girl on the block. We can witness that our spouse, or our mother, or our friend is in an unusually grumpy mood, and draw the conclusion that they are angry with us and that we are unloved. Anytime we are in a situation and draw a conclusion based on our beliefs and biases or upon insufficient evidence, we are in danger of harming ourselves by drawing disconnected conclusions. This negative mental habit is harmful to relationships; to our relationship with ourselves and our relationships with others.

The way to deal with the habit of making disconnected conclusions is to first recognize that you are making them. Evaluate a situation that you are uncomfortable about and pay attention to what you are saying to yourself *about yourself* in that circumstance. If your evaluation is negative, look at the evidence that supports the negative evaluation. Then, look at the evidence that supports the opposite evaluation. Find alternative explanations for the situation besides the explanation that supports your negative belief. Then, when you find that more evidence supports a more positive self-evaluation, *make a choice* to assume the more positive alternative.

So, if your best friend is unusually grumpy when you talk with her on the phone, do you conclude that you have done something to upset her? From that conclusion, do you decide that you are not a very good friend? Evaluate that thinking. What else is going on for your friend that has nothing whatever to do with you? Could the reality that she was talking on the phone with you while she was grumpy signify that she trusts you enough to share her grumpy mood with you? Do you have other friends? Are you the kind of friend that you would like to have? If your evaluation indicates that you are, in fact, the kind of friend you would like to have and if you can see that your friend has things to be grumpy about that are unrelated to you, your conclusion that you are not a very good friend could be disconnected from the realities of your friend's life and disconnected from your knowledge and skills about friendship. Do not let an isolated judgment color your whole opinion of yourself.

Selective negative focus   The next category of "muddy" thinking" is selective negative focus. Focusing selectively on the negatives, we take information out of context and ignore the whole picture in favor of focusing in on one non-representative detail. This way of thinking is beautifully illustrated whenever we get into perfectionist mode. A perfectionistic woman cannot tolerate the idea of making a mistake, because the mistake represents failure. Although she does many things very well, selective negative focus on imperfect performance means she has failed. The result is ongoing anxiety and negative feelings about herself.

When I was in junior college, working on my associate's degree, I studied one year of chemistry, calculus, and physics. In truth, it was the most challenging year of my college career. Prior to beginning my chemistry course, I enrolled in and successfully completed an introductory chemistry course. That introductory chemistry course successfully prepared me so that my first semester of college chemistry was fun and manageable. As I was accustomed to, I earned an "A" in the class. However, in my second semester of college chemistry, I was confronted with a more difficult challenge. I had enjoyed the pleasure of learning under the supervision of the same teacher for my introductory as well as my first semester chemistry course. I understood the "language" of my chemistry teacher and performed rather well. For second semester chemistry, the subject matter was much more challenging and I did not understand the new instructor as well as I had understood my first chemistry professor. About mid-semester, I took an exam for which I had prepared as I usually prepared (in a very conscientious manner) and earned a "D" on the exam. I was dumbfounded. For two or three hours, or maybe for the rest of the day, I walked around believing that I was stupid because I had earned a "D" on an exam. This is the perfect example of selective abstraction. I was an honor student. I graduated from that college with a 3.98 grade point average and "highest honors." In order for me to have walked around believing that I was stupid as a result of one exam, I had to ignore my performance during the rest of my junior college career.

Had I continued in my selective negative focus, I could have decided that I was too stupid to continue my college career. But I shook the belief that I was stupid off with the realization that I did not connect well with the second semester professor, that the work was more difficult, and that I was simply not cut out for chemistry. As a result, I was able to confidently move forward in school.

A more recent example in my own life occurs during my weekly piano lessons. I have a fabulous piano teacher, who is capable of training me until I reach a professional level of performance on the piano. Although piano is something that I dearly love and is an activity I regularly participate in to soothe myself, it is also a vehicle that I used to use to practice selective negative focus. A few years ago, my life was hectic and I had not been able to practice between lessons for two weeks. Hence, I attended two lessons feeling unprepared and experiencing guilt and shame for not being "good enough" or "serious enough" about my piano. I felt I was wasting my time and my teacher's time, so I told her what I was thinking and feeling, and I suggested that I quit my lessons until I had more time for practice. My teacher would not cooperate with that plan! She told me that she loved having me as her student, that she knew I was passionate about my music and that life *is* busy. She went on to convince me that every lesson is valuable, even without practice! In reality, my teacher reminded me of the things I had been selectively ignoring: that I was passionate about my music, that I was very good at the piano, and that just because life is busy, that is no reason for me to abandon my passion! Thank you, Debbie!

Overgeneralization — When we engage in overgeneralization, we use an isolated incident to serve as a representation of similar situations everywhere. This is an example of messages from our childhood that hold the potential to sneak up behind us and catch us unaware.

One example that comes to my mind is from my early experiences in public speaking. I had spoken at church events and addressed people publicly from the time I was about 12 years old. And so, as a therapist interested in increasing contact with potential clients, I eagerly agreed to speak with a group of school administrators in a district near my home. I prepared an icebreaker activity that would be fun and yet draw the interest of my audience toward the topic of my lecture. During the time I was mingling with my audience before my actual presentation, they seemed friendly and open. However, this was the worst audience that I had ever spoken to. They were answering cell phones and pagers and talking and laughing amongst themselves during my whole presentation. Even when I stopped my presentation to comment on the unruliness of the audience and ask for their cooperation, the laughter and rudeness continued! It felt like I was speaking to an auditorium full of children!

This experience shook me up a bit. I had to struggle with myself to resist the thought that all audiences everywhere would respond to me in-kind. My "muddy thinking" led me to believe that what I had to say to an audience was so off base or ridiculous that an audience would deem me unworthy of their time and even heckle me because of what I was saying. My overgeneralization could result in the conclusion that I should never speak again publicly because I engender such a negative response. A much more balanced thought is that perhaps I was having an off day; however, the audience was rude and inattentive. In fact, the administrator who had invited me to speak to them later apologized for their behavior, with some tonal indication that my experience with this group reflects the general candor of the group. Judging from the administrator's explanation, a more correct conclusion is that I was speaking to an overworked group of teachers who resented the requirement to attend a district meeting. Their unruly behavior was probably not directed toward me, but toward their district administrators. Therefore, the decision not to speak at a school district meeting again *might* be an overgeneralization, because I am making the decision based on one isolated experience. But if I were to cease my public speaking completely based on this experience, I would be limiting myself based on an isolated incident and getting myself stuck in the muddy thinking of overgeneralization.

In fact, overgeneralization is a favored pattern of muddy thinking among many women. This is specifically true with regard to the way we view our relationships with men. Here is an example that can illustrate my point. When I became of age to begin dating, I always arrived home at the end of the evening to find that my parents had left the porch light on for me. Even if they had already gone to bed, the porch light being left on came to represent a symbol that I was loved. When I got married, however, my new husband had no knowledge of my history with porch lights and was unaware of the symbolism of the porch light. So when I came home at night and he had not made a point to turn the light on when it got dark, I felt unloved. I had over-generalized my experience with the porch light while

I lived at home to mean that every porch light left burning after the sun went down signified that a loved one was being waited for at home, somewhat like the symbolism of a yellow ribbon tied around a tree. Because of this, I silently grumbled and *felt unloved* every time I came home to a darkened front porch. Then, when I revealed my feelings, and my (former) husband made the point that our porch was illuminated by the street light in front of our home, I felt doubly rejected.

This example leads me to think of another one. From time to time, I hear a woman exclaim: "All men are jerks!" I have also heard that they are all slobs, they are all lazy or they are all unfeeling. There are endless possibilities for what can be said about "all men." The problem is that whenever we say something about an entire group of people, it is an overgeneralization more commonly recognized as racism or sexism. Blanket statements like those I've described here are never universally true, although a particular woman's experiences may seem to indicate that all men fit in whatever category she may place them into. Many women who have had negative experiences with men that began in childhood form sexist beliefs based on their isolated negative experiences. When I make this explanation, I often get the response that a woman's experiences with men that led to these negative conclusion are not isolated because they represent all of her experiences with every man with whom she has had a close relationship. To these women, I explain that their experiences are isolated because there have only been abusive, controlling or negative men in their lives. The concept that loving, honest, loyal and gentle men exist is foreign because, once a woman has become old enough to "choose" with whom to relate, she only has the relationship skills for interacting with the same types of men who have been a part of her life until that point in time. The relationship skills she learned during abusive relationships growing up are the only skills she has when it comes to attracting men. With those skills, she only knows how to attract abusive men. The key to connecting with a different kind of person is to learn new ways of interacting that attract the kinds of relationships that are more nurturing and satisfying. Clearing up muddy thinking is an excellent start in that direction.

Blowing It Out of Proportion — When we Blow It Out of Proportion, we tend toward unreasonably exaggerating our qualities, whether they are good or bad. One significant way in which women do this is by focusing too much on some aspect of the way they look. If a little pimple on your nose keeps you from going to a PTA meeting or to church, you are probably blowing it out of proportion! Ok, you say, it isn't a little pimple, it is the size of the Empire State Building! So, what are you worried about? Think that everyone who sees you will look at you and use that pimple to draw conclusions about who you are? Yes, perhaps they will look at you and believe you are a slob, that you never wash your face and that you are too ugly to interact with—but that usually is not the case! When we make a negative evaluation of ourselves then focus on it, we unfairly disadvantage ourselves because we assume that others are judging us as critically as we judge ourselves. It simply is not true. And, if someone does make a negative evaluation based on a superficial detail, life has just provided us with an opportunity to practice not giving our power away to a minor detail or to a negative person.

Another characteristic women typically blow out of proportion is weight and body shape. We live in a weight-conscious society and the interesting thing is that underweight women, average women, fabulously fit women, deliciously curvaceous women and overweight women all have this pattern of muddy thinking in common. Many, many of us use our weight to determine our value. That way of thinking sabotages us because we can become so biased that two or three or ten or fifty pounds or more come to represent who we are to the exclusion of positive qualities, gifts and talents that enhance our lives. Blowing weight and body shape out of proportion blinds us to our strengths. It can also create distance in our relationships when our focus is so much on our own appearance as to prevent us from focusing on the enjoyment of our families, spouses and friends.

If weight or health issues present valid concerns that need addressing, why not do something about it without allowing it to become the focus of life? Just make healthy eating and exercise part of the daily routine. De-emphasize it. You might start a diet and exercise program, but do not let it become your focus so much that you encourage others to focus on it, too. Do not announce that you are "on a diet" or "working out" in social settings unless you are also willing to announce that you took your shower today! We would be so much the better if we focus our energy, instead, on getting to know other people and learning more about how to live our lives to the fullest. Another way to illustrate to yourself how far you have blown concerns about weight out of proportion is to ask yourself this question: "What else would I have time to do or to enjoy if I was not so consumed with my body?" Do not allow the habit of being overly concerned about your weight rob you of the joy you can experience in life!

We can also blow it out of proportion when we focus on mistakes we make. I used to have this funny habit that signaled me whenever I was blowing something out of proportion. Most often, it happened when I was thinking back over something I had said or done. It always occurred when I was alone and always came with the muddy thought that I was stupid. The most recent example occurred just after my current husband underwent open-heart surgery. Before the surgery, I had booked a speaking engagement at a local church that I thought I would be able to follow-through with – it was scheduled for the day after my husband's surgery. The stress of that time prevented me from realizing that I probably would not be up to giving a presentation the day after seeing my husband coming out of surgery and supporting him through the processes involved in such a major trauma. During that time, I was surrounded by supportive friends and family who had questioned me from the moment they knew that I had booked the speaking engagement. Unfortunately, I did not agree that I was incapable of public speaking at that time, until the day after the surgery—the same day I was to speak! One of my girlfriends took it upon herself to call and cancel for me. As might be expected, the woman who had booked me was not very happy about the last minute cancellation and she verbalized that to my friend. I was exhausted, though, and could not have gone, in spite of my desire to do it. So I felt a great deal of relief. But when I was alone and had a chance to evaluate myself and blow the single incident of last minute cancellation that I had ever been responsible for out of proportion, I blurted out with a loud, sing-song "La-la-la!" Following the impulsive song, I began obsessing about what I had done wrong, and how I would never be booked for a speaking engagement again. Truly, I was blowing the situation out of proportion.

Finding myself blurting out a "La-la-la!" was my signal that I was thinking about something excessively and negatively. The impulsive song was represented a "heads-up" that I was obsessing and that I was making a compulsive attempt to block my discomfort about the negative thoughts running through my head. The song also represented an invitation for me to explore my thoughts and correct them so that I could feel better about the situation. This anecdote provides an example of how muddy thinking is often accompanied by compulsive behavior. Whenever we find ourselves doing something we do not want to do, but feel compelled to do, it is worthwhile to evaluate our thoughts. There is usually a pattern of thinking that coincides with the impulse to do something we do not wish to do or that brings us harm.

A very common pattern of muddy thinking surfaces when I encourage a woman to attend to her own needs. When I suggest, for example, that the young mother eat regularly even though that may interrupt the pace of activity her family is used to, her response, many times, is that such behavior is selfish. Nobody wants to think of herself as selfish, especially if she was encouraged to share as a child, with the implication that "little girls who do not share are bad." Here is something to think about; being a little selfish is a good thing. This is especially true if our attempts at self-care are labeled selfish by anyone with whom we relate on a daily basis. In my first marriage, I was called selfish whenever I locked the bathroom door to enjoy a bath with music and candlelight (about once every six months!). Insisting on good self-care, even though others are calling you selfish, reinforces the reality that you are of value for yourself, even if others do not get the concept. And, if you are in a relationship that consistently requires you to de-value yourself, being selfish from time to time begins to break the pattern that keeps you stuck in the mud of an oppressive situation. So do not allow isolated incidents of self-care behavior to be blown out of proportion to mean that you are a selfish person. In fact, do just the opposite: do *more* self care behaviors if your self-care is being called selfish. Most likely, you are being labeled selfish because the person complaining about your self-care benefits from you not attending to your own needs, even though ignoring your own needs is detrimental and draining for you.

Just one final word on blowing it out of proportion. Have you ever had a bad hair day or come home from a meeting to discover you had a booger hanging visibly in your nostril? Did you take that bad hair or that booger to mean you are a loser and no one cares to interact with a loser? Ask yourself this question: "Did anyone run, screaming, from my presence?" If they did not, you should probably not focus on something that undermines the reality that you are a worthwhile individual. Most likely, it is a small thing, and the good news is that everybody has boogers!

Shrinking the Significance — The opposite muddy thinking habit from Blowing It Out of Proportion is Shrinking the Significance of a situation. How did you respond the last time you were paid a compliment? Did you acknowledge the truth of what was being said by simply responding with "Thank you?" Or did you disagree with the person who paid you the compliment? If you disagreed, you are probably in the habit of shrinking the significance of your value and contributions. This is one of my personal habits of muddy thinking, and it does limit my potential, by disallowing the positive observations of others who are encouraging me in the direction of my goals. This is how it works. About a year ago, I was visiting with a few women and the conversation turned to how I earn my living. That question always leads to my response that although I am a therapist, my aspiration is to become a published author. Then, I usually say that I have seven books completely outlined "in my head." As usual, this group of women wanted to know about each book and, as I explained my ideas and how they would develop for each book, the women began to compliment me on my creativity and to encourage me to write. My response to them was typical muddy thinking. I said: "Yeah, I should." The enthusiasm I met with in this conversation and others like it usually resulted in my walking away from the situation thinking about how large the task of writing is, and how I am not smart or creative enough to write in a way that anyone would care to read. This way of thinking completely diminished the significance of the enthusiasm others had for my ideas. That enthusiasm could have caused me to think: "Wow, women get excited about my ideas! I should write them down because people will buy my books!" I actually have several clients on my "Please let us know when your book comes out" list. They make that request because they value what I have taught them and they want more. Should I allow muddy thinking to shrink the significance of such requests and never put my ideas on paper? Of course not.

Another way I shrink the significance of situations is common to many women. My new husband tells me on a daily basis that I am beautiful. He even uses "beautiful" as a nickname for me. That has been tough for me! Although I have always tried to look my best, to have someone acknowledge beauty in me broke an internal rule I had that "beautiful" was not okay for me. My new husband could sense that whenever he called me beautiful, he made me cringe. So, in a typical fashion of someone who loves you and wants you to understand something good about yourself, my response led him to tell me all the more. He began saying, "You *are* beautiful, you know." I was so uncomfortable with this that I began responding with "Okay, okay!" or "Stop!" Finally, a friend of mine teamed up with my husband and together, they encouraged me to playfully stroke my brow and say "Thank you!" The interesting thing is that after a little practice, I discovered that it was not such a big deal. It is okay to be beautiful and to accept a compliment with a thank you. It is not conceit to simply express gratitude for a compliment.

But the interesting thing is that I had unconsciously taught my daughters a mixed message about what to do with a compliment. One afternoon, I told my oldest daughter that the top she was wearing was really cute. She said: "Isn't it?" in agreement with me. I responded by telling her that when someone compliments her, she should not agree, but should just say thanks. I had experienced discomfort about her frank acceptance of a compliment, so I told her that her response was rude. She responded by saying: "That's what you say, mom." She was right! This interaction caused me to realize that although there is nothing wrong with accepting a compliment by agreeing with it, I had made an *emotional decision* to avoid accepting compliments is such a way for fear of losing acceptance from others. The irony here is that just the opposite is true. Accepting compliments with a thank you or by agreeing makes other people feel more comfortable because their observations are acknowledged rather than dismissed.

Let us acknowledge rather than shrink the significance of our own value. We will be better and happier for it.

Personalization — This pattern of muddy thinking involves blaming ourself for events that fall outside of personal control. During childhood, we developed patterns of behavior and thinking that helped us to avoid personal discomfort. Particularly, when we perceived that our need for food or emotional or physical safety was threatened, we used our own behavior to attempt to get what we needed. In short, we made attempts to manipulate (with behaviors like crying, trying to please the parent, or throwing a tantrum, for example) a parent into giving us what we needed. Consequently, one of the errors we made in childhood was developing the belief that by being "good enough" or "cute enough" or "funny enough" or by doing whatever appeared to please or cause discomfort for the parent whom was the focus of our concern, we controlled that parent. Sometimes, this belief led us to conclude that we could actually stop someone from harming us or cause that person to love us. The reality that we failed to acknowledge as a child was that it was terrifying to imagine that a person to whom we looked for our very childhood survival might not have been concerned enough to see that our basic needs were met. Or that the parent actually wanted to cause us harm. Think, for example, of the behavior of a small child that has been denied a snack when he or she is hungry because "dinner is almost ready." That child's world falls apart and he or she whines and cries and focuses an incredible amount of intense energy on the parent who is requesting another ten minutes to get dinner on the table. To a child's way of thinking, ten minutes of waiting to eat feels as catastrophic as the possibility of never being able to eat again. To a child, being refused food does not lead to the adult logic of "I can wait a few minutes." Rather, it leads to "I am *never* going to eat!" To the child's perception, it is a real threat to survival! This child's mother may pay close attention to meeting her child's nutritional needs and she may do a good job fulfilling those needs. Nonetheless, in the child's perception the mother is not vigilant enough.

However, for the child to acknowledge her perception that her survival is dependent on a person who is not vigilant enough to fulfill her needs would mean that the child's survival seems to be threatened on a regular basis. A safer belief for the child would be to develop the idea that the child can *control* the mother in order to ensure that the child's needs are met. To do that, the child develops a pattern of behaviors with the intention to control, whether those behaviors include being good or cute or funny or cantankerous. This strategy works very well during childhood, because a child cannot focus on developmental tasks required in growing up if that child is pre-occupied with whether or not her parent will attend to her survival that day. However, this survival tactic does not work very well in adulthood. As an example, one of the ways I earned my kudos while I grew up was by cleaning the house. If I felt threatened in any way, I just kicked into "please my parent" mode and cleaned the house. It usually resulted in a better mood for my parent and increased feelings of security for me. When I got married, the strategy did not work as well. I had unconsciously become very adept throughout my growing up years at watching the faces of people I depended on in order to anticipate their moods. I did this with my spouse, as well. During my first year of marriage, I used to look at my husband's face and think he was mad at me. If that was my thought, I kicked into high gear and began cleaning the house. Every time! I spent an extraordinary amount of time cleaning, until one day when I realized what I was doing. I was fearfully cleaning the kitchen, hoping that he would not express his anger toward me. Then, I stopped. I thought, "I think he is mad and I am cleaning the house?! That does not make any sense!" And, I realized that I really had not done anything to make him angry. So I took a deep breath and approached him to ask if he was angry with me. I found out that he was not angry with *me*, but that he was angry. By assuming that I had caused his anger and that I could rectify it by my action of cleaning the house, I had personalized the situation.

Think of the last time a friend or someone you work with was angry. Did you assume that you did something to make her angry? As women, we tend to move straight from an observation that someone close to us is having a negative emotion to "what did I do?" mode. Most of the time, the mood has very little to do with us. To break this bad habit, practice assuming that another person's foul mood is a result of circumstances unrelated to you, unless that person comes to you to specifically identify something you have done to offend. And, even then, be careful not to accept blame for the other person's negative feelings after you have taken responsibility for your part in the problem. Remember, everyone *chooses* how to respond to others within the context of a relationship and if someone you interact with chooses to hold onto grudges, simply allow that person to remain miserable with that choice. You do not have to take it on, too.

All-or-Nothing Thinking — You may be familiar with the next type of "muddy thinking." It has several labels: either/or thinking, black-or-white thinking, or all-or-nothing thinking. This is the mantra that if you are going to do something, you must do it right, or not do it at all. If something is not completely right, it is wrong. This kind of thinking makes perfection the goal and anything less than perfection unacceptable. This is the mentality we maintain when we eat a cookie, then decide we've "blown it" and proceed to abandon good nutrition habits the rest of the day or week or month. If you are in the habit of saying, "I'll start my diet again on Monday," you are probably doing all-or-nothing thinking. This thinking does not allow for mistakes or for the experience of being human. It is much better to realize that our humanity requires that we make mistakes. This is how we learn. So after the cookie, evaluate the situation. Did you enjoy every bite? Or did you scarf it down without tasting it? If you swallowed it without chewing it, your object becomes to learn from the cookie. What emotions were you having that triggered you to reach for soothing in a cookie? Figure that out and you can recognize the same trigger next time, *before* you eat the cookie. Then, you have learned from the experience and do not have to label yourself a failure because you ate one cookie. Even if you ate six cookies or more before stopping to evaluate the emotional triggers leading up to the cookies, the process can still be effective. They key is in evaluating and looking for what you can learn, rather than in rejecting yourself during the learning process.

All-or-nothing muddy thinking has an insidious effect on our willingness to try new things. It can influence us to believe we cannot do something that we have not even tried because of fear of failing and the belief that something that isn't done perfectly isn't worth doing. Just like a cookie can lead to the conclusion that an entire day is ruined in terms of healthy eating, so can an art project be abandoned because the artist sees a single "flaw" which, in reality, represents the individuality and beauty of the work to others who admire the art. Apply this idea to anything you avoid doing because you think you do not do it well enough. Does your desire for perfection and your tendency toward self-rejection if something isn't good enough limit your willingness to try new things? The ability to work at something and to accept the concept that growth occurs within the context of improving at something you have not yet mastered provides the avenue for positive development of the self and growth in confidence. It requires an enjoyment of the process of learning without the judgment or self-criticism that all-or-nothing muddy thinking inspires.

Finally, a word about the effects of all-or-nothing muddy thinking on our relationships. Conflict is common to every relationship since relationships are developed between people whose needs will not always coincide. The presence of conflict in relationships requires that participants be able to deal with conflict as it arises in constructive ways that lead to the mutual satisfaction of conflicting needs. Difficulty arises, however, if all-or-nothing thinking influences one or both of the relationship participants. This kind of thinking also prevents us from processing problems that surface in relationships when we believe that we are not good at interactions, rather than seeing a current problem as a temporary stalemate and trusting ourselves to be able to work through it. We might say something like: "We can't solve this problem, so I'm not even going to try" or "I can't talk to my partner, so I'm just going to ignore the problem and maybe it will go away." Conflict in relationships does not disappear when it is ignored. Conflict does require an ongoing willingness to work with difficulties and to tolerate the reality that even though a solution to a conflict does not emerge during the first discussion of the conflict, the absence of a solution does not mean the conflict is not near a compromise. Keep working at it and tolerate the ambivalence associated with an unresolved conflict long enough to reason the problem through. Avoid the tendency to say a solution cannot be found if the solution is neither perfect nor instantaneous.

Labeling — Another form of "muddy thinking" is the habit of attaching a fixed, global label on yourself or others. Most of the time, labeling has a negative effect when we make a mistake. We see this kind of muddy thinking most often when a parent is correcting a child. To say "good girl" when the child has done something that pleases the parent or "bad girl" when the child has made a mistake is to teach her that if she *does* something good, she *is* good, but, if she does something bad, she *is* bad. This is where feelings of shame come from. If you often experience feelings of shame, or think you are bad when you make a mistake, think back to those times your parent told you that you were bad. Recognize that if you displeased your parent, you went against your parent's value system, but what you were doing may not have been a bad choice in the context of what you understand to be right or wrong from an adult perspective. For example, if you were told you were bad during or after being sexually abused, that label came from your parent's refusal to take personal responsibility for their evil behavior. For you, accepting the label helped you survive better than you would have been able to if you had come to the conscious realization that someone you depended upon was willing to hurt you in that way.

The message that a choice makes a person bad need not involve such an extreme situation, however. Something as seemingly benign as having been called a "bad girl" for spilling milk can translate into feeling ashamed when other simple mistakes are committed. If you are in the habit of calling yourself or others bad for making mistakes, develop the habit of recognizing that making a mistake does not make a person bad. Mistakes occur during the process of learning and are natural, common and expected as a result of living. Also, keep in mind that "bad" is not the only label we assign to mistakes. Any negative label fits this category of muddy thinking. For example, we might have the habit of calling ourselves "lazy," "stupid" or "selfish" in response to mistakes we make or decisions we make which might be contrary to those things we were taught during childhood, but which don't necessarily apply well to our adult circumstances. More will be explained about invalid childhood mandates when I discuss imperatives.

Tunnel Vision — Tunnel vision involves seeing only what we want to see or what is consistent with our worldview. This method of "muddy thinking" precludes alternative possibilities or explanations for situations, usually based on a strong emotional need to maintain a belief system that provides emotional safety. To illustrate this method of muddy thinking, let me introduce you to Tessa. Tessa is an attractive, intelligent 24-year-old daughter of first generation Eastern European immigrants. Her parents came to the United States in the 1950's and have worked hard doing menial labor until Tessa's father was able to successfully purchase and operate a sandwich shop. Owing to the difficulty Tessa witnessed in her family as her parents struggled to make ends meet, she concluded that obtaining a college education would prevent her and her future family from struggling in the manner she had as a child because of financial obstacles. The problem Tessa encounters with this way of thinking is that Tessa's parents are disappointed with her determination to rebel against tradition and seek something else for herself besides finding a good, hard-working Eastern European boy to settle down and make babies with. To them, a self-supporting woman or one who works outside the home confronts tradition in a manner that causes them to conclude that Tessa is rebellious and disrespectful toward her heritage. Tessa's parents illustrate the "muddy thinking" of tunnel vision with their refusal to see Tessa's choice to educate herself as a respectable option since it falls outside the tradition established for generations within her family. Because of her family's response, Tessa would do well to monitor herself so as to avoid falling into muddy thinking, especially Labeling. She might have a subconscious belief, based on her childhood upbringing and her parents' response to her current choices that she is selfish for seeking a college education. Tessa and her family illustrate how muddy thinking is propagated through generations. Tessa's responsibility is to recognize that her family's beliefs do not apply to her personal situation and move forward with her plans, monitoring her thoughts to be sure that she goes forward confidently while avoiding muddy thinking patterns.

Biased Explanations — This is a habit of muddy thinking that I often discover when working with couples to improve their relationships. It occurs when we find negative explanations for someone else's behavior without reference to the other person's experience or motivation. It involves suspicious thinking that assumes negative ulterior motives on the part of one's mate. Let me introduce you to Barry and Sandra. They have been married six years and have a four-year-old daughter. Barry works for the railroad and Sandra is a freelance artist. During Sandra's childhood, her parents divorced following many arguments regarding her father's multiple affairs. Because of the nature of his work, Barry is gone from the family home frequently for periods of four or five days at a time. This worries Sandra, but she is able to soothe herself regarding Barry's fidelity based on his willingness to provide her with a work schedule and his punctual arrival at home at the end of his shift. However, a few weeks before Sandra's birthday, Barry stops coming home punctually. He arrives home about two hours late every day because he is taking the time after work to search for a birthday gift that will please and surprise his wife. Because he wants to surprise her, he gives a brief comment about extra safety meetings at work in response to her queries regarding his punctuality. Sandra is becoming increasingly worried, tense and suspicious. Although she resists the urge to openly accuse Barry, she believes he is having an affair. Her opinion is not based on reality. She is creating negative assumptions without reference to Barry's experiences.

In reality, there are several possible explanations for Barry's tardiness, including the fact that he is shopping for her birthday, that he is actually attending meetings at the close of his shift or that the train schedules have been delayed due to unusual circumstances. But Sandra is unlikely to consider alternative possibilities because of her habit of entertaining biased explanations. It would serve Sandra well to explore her thoughts and feelings regarding her belief that Barry is likely to be unfaithful because her father was. If Sandra could recognize that she has a biased assumption based on her childhood experience, she would be more able to question that assumption and look for alternate possibilities for Barry's behavior. The important concept to recognize in this situation is that when Sandra is able to entertain multiple possibilities in her mind as to her spouse's behaviors, she is far less likely to inquire about his behavior or express her concerns about his tardiness in a way that causes him to become defensive. If the only possibility she can conceive is that he is having an affair, her inquiry is likely to become accusatory and to cause an argument.

Biased explanations frequently occur because of difficult previous experiences and an absence of objective curiosity about other's motivations. If this is a pattern of "muddy thinking" you engage in regularly, consider identifying your underlying belief that drives the need to assume negative intentions on the part of others. Where did you learn that you could not trust someone close to you? Once you identify the situation in which your belief that others will hurt you was developed, you will be able to more objectively evaluate new situations without reference to prior experiences. You will be able to do this by comparing the person in question with the person in your past that was hurtful to you. If they are similar, you may need to look more closely at the relationship and explore the possibilities for healing together. If the two individuals are dissimilar, you would do well to remind yourself of the differences between the two in support of the concept that they probably do not share the motivation to cause you harm.

Mind Reading — Mind reading is a pattern of muddy thinking that women have made famous! It involves the expectation that our spouse should have the magical ability to know what we are thinking without the benefit of verbal communication. It sounds something like this: "If you loved me, you would know that I need a massage when I say my neck is stiff. I shouldn't have to ask you do rub my neck!" Mind reading is also frequently in play when you finish your partner's sentence or when he finishes yours. It is the pattern of muddy thinking that prompts us to say: "I know what you are going to say" or "I know what you are thinking."

In reality, healthy relationships have no room for mind reading. It may come as a shock to some people, but love is not synonymous with the ability to know what someone needs or wants without communicating those needs or wants verbally. Imagine that every time you said, "I'm hungry," your partner went to the kitchen and prepared you something to eat without inquiring as to what you were hungry for. Perhaps you are hungry for popcorn and you are offered some yogurt. You never communicate what you are hungry for, but each time your partner brings you food that isn't what you had in mind, you feel unloved because your partner did not satisfy your craving. As ridiculous as it sounds, when we expect our partner to mind read, we apply this kind of thinking and expect our partner to know our history and changing needs. Then, we feel rejected or unloved because our partner is not omniscient. In my experience, it is difficult enough for people to understand and correctly identify *their own* needs. Thus, the task of correctly identifying and meeting your partner's needs without communication about those needs is next to impossible. Equating love with the ability to mind read is a romantic notion that has no place in healthy relationships. Some couples would argue that in the beginning of their relationship, they were able to successfully read each other's minds and intuit each other's needs. I would label that exception as the happy serendipity that is part of the coupling process when each partner is so focused on being liked by the other that each gives based on personal needs and those personal needs happen to match well. It is part of the process that drives a couple to commit to each other. It is a necessary process, but not an indication of how the relationship will proceed, once the commitment is established. Following commitment, clear communication and dedication to helping each other grow are necessary if the relationship is to flourish.

As already mentioned, mind reading also includes predicting what someone else is thinking or saying. This habit takes the place of listening. If you believe you know ahead of time what someone is going to say, I would suggest adopting a more curious position and spending more time in the practice of listening. It is irritating and disrespectful to the person who is speaking when we "check out" of the conversation by predicting what is being communicated and responding to what we predicted rather than what is actually being said.

Thinking With Your Feelings — This muddy thinking habit comes from making decisions about ourselves and others based on how we feel. The soundest decisions are made as we balance our feelings about a situation with reasoning about the concrete, objective facts. We all hold beliefs that *feel* true to us, but which are not objectively true. The most salient example I can recall comes from work I did in my own psychotherapy. I don't recall what I had been talking about, but I must have been berating myself for something, when my therapist interrupted me with a piercing question: "Are you good?" His question jolted me and sent intense feelings throughout my body. I didn't answer his question. He just sat, not even blinking, and asked me again: "Are you good?" Finally, I answered: "No." I felt as if I had just unmasked myself and shown him that my core was rotten. I felt shame and embarrassment to have been exposed like that. I was overwhelmed with feelings of being "bad." But, as soon as I said "No," he responded with: "Prove it. Convince me that you are not good." It was in that moment in time when I began the struggle to differentiate between something that *feels* true and something that is actually true. In reality, I was and am very good. I searched my memory to find evidence that I was bad. I could find none in spite of the compelling strength of feeling that I was not good. I had allowed feelings about myself to create reality for me. I was thinking with my feelings. The feelings were based on negative, critical evaluations of me made by others – others who did not have authority or appropriate insight about me to make those evaluations.

Thinking with our feelings is the pattern of thinking that compels us to believe that just because we are afraid of something, we should avoid that thing. I used to have a fear of singing for audiences. Whenever I was invited to sing for a church audience, my beliefs about myself and my fear about singing were so strong that I shook. That shaking caused a quivering in my diaphragm that made it impossible for me to properly support and project my voice. I lacked confidence and that came across whenever I attempted to sing in front of an audience. My fear was inspiring me to draw incorrect conclusions (thinking with fear). I concluded that there were other singers in my audience who sang better than I did, so no one really wanted to hear me sing. That belief really *felt* true. I was so dismayed at the reality that I could sing beautifully alone but not in public that I began to explore my thoughts and feelings to discover a more objective explanation about singing in public. I realized that although there were others who sang better than I did, that did not mean that my talent was invalid. I also recognized that there were people who loved to hear me sing. They told me so. Once I realized those things, I *made the choice* to ignore the fear and focus on the realities. Now, I am invited to sing for church audiences and I think it is fun. I can now sing as well in church as I ever did alone. I am a confident, talented singer, but I did not become one until I stopped allowing myself to draw conclusions based upon my fear.

I challenged the fear. Fear is usually an illusion. Most of the time, when we confront fear, we discover that it dissolves and that we have more talent, strength, courage and knowledge than the fear would allow us to see.

A very important point about thinking with our feelings is that any time we avoid doing something that we want to do or when we continuously find ourselves unsuccessful at something we know how to do, we must recognize that we are probably thinking with our feelings. We are allowing ourselves to be limited by the feeling reality of a situation. When that happens, it is super important to evaluate those things that feel true, but are not. Usually, invalid beliefs that feel true come from childhood experiences. To objectively evaluate them, it is useful to seek the opinion of someone you trust, who is capable of helping you see clearly the difference between past realities and current situations. This person could be a trusted friend whom you know always speaks the truth to you in a way that inspires you to confront your fears and be your best self. If you do not have a friend like this, seek professional counseling; it is well worth the effort, time and money.

Imperatives — Imperatives are the rules we follow which are based in fear or guilt. When I think of these rules, I think of the things we feel we "should" do because that is what a good wife, mother, employee, etc. does. It is also the thing we choose to do or not to do based upon the question: "What will the neighbors think?" Imperatives are anxiety-driven. Often, imperatives are outside of conscious awareness until a situation occurs that pressures us to challenge the imperative. For example, for many of us who have ever struggled with weight issues, an imperative exists that we should not waste food. In the family I grew up in, I had a beloved grandmother who insisted upon feeding everyone who came through her front door hungry. She was nurturing and loving and I never heard her speak a cross word. However, she had a very clear rule that the children must eat everything on their plates. Children were also encouraged to load their own plates at grandma's house, but in response to "Can I have more?" there was always the response "Yes, but if you put it on your plate, you have to eat it." Whether the imperative is in this form or in the "children are starving in Africa" form, the imperative exerts itself in the moment when our belly tells us that we are full, but we ignore our body signals in order to honor our membership in the "Clean Plate Club." To overcome the imperatives, we must commit ourselves to being conscious of our choices and choosing to honor ourselves even when we feel anxiety pressuring us to make unhealthy choices. In order to stop ourselves from overeating in the situation I have described here, we have to be willing to listen to our body signals that tell us we are full, and to confront the anxiety that arises with the possibility of wasting food. When we have been able to consistently manage the anxiety enough to allow our body signals to dictate how much we eat, we will have made great strides toward "growing up" where eating is concerned. When we consistently focus on becoming aware of and confronting imperatives, the patterns of thinking that drive unhealthy or compulsive behavior come into our awareness and we are able to make direct, conscious decisions which will support our functioning as autonomous adults.

Giving Your Power Away — This pattern of muddy thinking is in play whenever we believe that someone else can make us do or feel something. As in: "You're making me mad." It is what happens when we respond emotionally to someone else's emotional expressions. For example, think of the last time someone was angry with you. How did you respond? For most of us, the automatic response is to also become angry, or to become fearful or nervous enough that our behavior becomes directed by whatever emotions we are experiencing in response to the other person's emotions. The example I used during my discussion of "Personalization" wherein I began cleaning the house when I thought my husband was angry is a good example of giving my power away. In fact, each pattern of muddy thinking that leads to behavior that would have worked during childhood, but no longer has validity in adult situations is an example of giving power away. Ideally, each time we act, it should be an action of choice. That is, we should be able to consciously choose our behaviors based on reason and upon evaluating the situation at hand. Every choice made compulsively because of an emotion we are trying to avoid is self-sabotage. It is giving our power away. This applies to those behaviors we perform when we are alone as well as those we do in reaction to someone else.

Overreacting to someone who makes a negative comment is another example of giving our power away. It is based on lack of insight that such comments come from the perspective of the comment maker, and may have very little to do with you. For example, one of my hobbies is creating stylish and unique clothing for myself. I truly enjoy making unique fashion statements. One of the dresses I made for myself is a vintage circa 1950's red dress with a tie waist and stand-up collar. I wear the dress with a chiffon petticoat and a lovely red crystal necklace. When I wear it, women frequently ask where I purchased the dress. When, with a twinkle in my eye, I say that I got it at the fabric store, they are disappointed that they cannot go shopping and purchase a dress like mine. However, one comment about my dress came from a guy who provided me the opportunity to retain my power, although it was a challenge for me! I went to church feeling beautiful in my red dress and he said: "What's with the Elvis collar?" It wasn't a compliment. I stood there for a moment, and then replied: "Because I can." I think he had expected me to feel humiliated by his question. He responded with surprise and restated my response: "Because you can?" I simply said, "Yes, because I can!" and walked away. If that had been the end of the exchange, I would have successfully avoided giving my power away. But, the exchange did not end when I walked away. I became angry in response to his critical question. I continued to think about it and to develop responses in my imagination to his rude intrusion. I played the interaction in my head over and over again, trying different responses in efforts to assert my value and to validate the privilege of creating my own style.

The next week, he made a point of approaching me to say: "No Elvis collar today, eh?" My response: "No, but if I had, it would have been perfectly fine!" What I *wanted* to do was to lay into him with a critical analysis of his personality and his own apparent discomfort with a woman who was not conforming to whatever standards of "appropriateness" he held in his own expectations! I also wanted to inform him that if he were to pay as much attention to his wife as he paid to my "Elvis collar," he might have had a successful relationship! Clearly, he had pressed my buttons! In fact, on three or four other occasions during the ensuing months, I would have chosen that same red dress to wear to church, except that his uninvited criticism remained with me and intimidated me. It wasn't until I became conscious about the reality that I was allowing this guy to influence my choice of what to wear to church that I realized I had been giving my power away. At that point, I stopped and reasoned the situation through. I concluded that this was a guy who had no idea of how to talk to women, much less how to pay a compliment. I decided that whatever his agenda was, it did not apply to me. Furthermore, I decided that if my freedom of personal expression made him uncomfortable enough to make rude comments, that it was *his* problem and *not* mine. The next Sunday morning, I boldly put on my red dress, and my husband and I sat in the pew directly in front of the uninvited critic and said not a word. Yes. I had taken my power back because I refused to allow an emotional response (intimidation) to influence my behavior (my choice of what to wear to church).

To avoid giving our power away, we must be able to differentiate between the feelings we experience in response to external events– our "old buttons" – and a rational evaluation of the situation at hand. Once we recognize the differences, we must consciously separate little kid feelings from our evaluation of the situation and make our decisions about how we will respond to another person based on the rational evaluation.

Returning to the metaphor of pulling ourselves out of the mud, the stones in the mud represent beliefs which, unexamined, cause pain and make breaking patterns of abuse particularly difficult. In order to pull ourselves out, we must understand where the stones are and recognize them for what they are. To do that, we must listen intently to our inner voice and pay attention to which patterns of muddy thinking we are practicing.

So, What Are You Going To Do About It?

By this point, you have identified your dreams and also identified some of the blocks you experience that prevent you from joyfully and relentlessly pursuing your dreams. Undoubtedly, you have recognized yourself in some of the examples of muddy thinking outlined in this chapter.

Here is your assignment:

Look at the homework you have created so far. Listen to the objections that come up when you dare to allow yourself to dream. Now, identify all of the patterns of muddy thinking you participate in that sabotage you. Journal about them. Remember, you cannot change muddy thinking unless you first recognize it and identify it as invalid to your current abilities and value. If you cannot identify the patterns of muddy thinking while you sit here considering the ideas in this chapter, make a point of listening to the things you say to yourself about yourself when you are alone and while you interact with others. When you discover some of your muddy thinking patterns, journal about them; if you simply take mental note and never write them down or process them, they are likely to slip back "under the radar" of your awareness, where they can continue to direct your behavior away from your own goals, dreams and desires.

CHAPTER 4

RECOGNIZING THE PIGPEN

Stop Letting Other People Keep You Stuck

Another way to think of emancipation is to imagine a pigpen. Sometimes, established patterns of interaction, although familiar, are like the wallow and mud of a pigpen. Pigs love their pens. They coat themselves in the mud, lie in it and enjoy the cool that it brings them. The mud is comfortable and familiar. The stench is the smell of home that brings comfort like a freshly baked batch of cookies. I would imagine that if pigs could talk, they would compliment each other on how nice they looked all caked in mud.

Now, imagine that you are a pig and live in the pen with other pigs. One day, you realize that there is more to life than wallowing in mud and waste. In fact, you have heard what some call a fairy tale; that there are actually pigs that live in houses with people, where they enjoy the affection of humans and the luxury of regular bathing and fresh table scraps. You begin to imagine yourself as a beautiful, well-groomed, sweet-smelling creature. You imagine what your life could be like outside of the pigpen. You tell your friends, the other pigs. They respond to your daydreams by telling you how good you look and smell covered in mud and waste. Why would you want to let your skin dry out? What would ever make you think you could be happy outside of the pen? Why would a pig want anything except the glorious wallow and delicious slop? At first, your aspirations for escaping the pigpen are met by amused curiosity, and then you are dismissed as being silly and nonsensical.

But there is something about life beyond the pigpen that calls to you. You decide to see what it would be like to stay out of the wallow. You refuse to let go of your vision beyond the pigpen and, as often happens when the universe recognizes a striving for something more, the farmer decides to wash down the pigs and showers you with a refreshing spray from the hose that frees you of mud and filth. You enjoy the feeling of your shower, and bask in the warmth of the sun on your clean hide.

As time passes, and you continue to entertain your dream of self-improvement, the other pigs become uncomfortable. Your yearnings to live beyond the limits imposed upon you seem to imply that life in the mire isn't good enough for you. Your friends assume that if this life isn't good enough for you, then, you must also think that *they* are not good enough for you either. Although your yearnings have nothing to do with the worthiness of your acquaintances, they feel judged and criticized by your longing for something beyond the pigpen. From their places of discomfort, they do everything in word and deed to discourage and isolate you. You become disheartened and begin to second-guess your aspirations beyond your current life.

One sunny afternoon, you sit just outside the mud, feeling the warmth of the sun while evaluating the wisdom of your daydreams. An old sow comes over and sits down next to you.

She is usually silent, but today gives you a few simple words of wisdom. "There are only two kinds of pigs in this world. There are those who believe that life is for living, breathing and feeling alive in those moments that challenge each of us to be the best pig we can be. These pigs are alive. Truly alive. The other kind of pigs are half-asleep: they are the 'walking dead.' They are lulled by the sludge they bathe in until they are scarcely aware of the flies swarming around their faces. These pigs end up on the dinner table. What kind of pig are you?"

This metaphor of the pigpen isn't far from the truth of how we live in our human relationships. The mud of the pigpen represents those patterns of interaction that encourage us to avoid growth, self-awareness and striving to become our best selves. It is quite a usual occurrence, when someone strives to attain or maintain higher moral ground, for those around them to exert pressure to "relax" or "don't be so uptight," in order to gain allegiance to some self-serving goal. It reminds me of an experience I had while newly divorced and just re-entering the world of dating. One guy, in particular, whom I did not know well, made several efforts to manipulate me into situations that would cause me to be alone with him. While out dancing with friends, he asked for a ride home (two hours out of my way) because, he told me, he had carpooled and would not be able to go back and get his car, as the people he had come with had already left for the night. I begrudgingly consented, and became more and more concerned as he talked about his new "make-out couch" during the drive to his apartment. When we arrived, I was too tired to drive safely the two hours to my home, so I locked myself into his child's bedroom and slept a few hours - just until I was certain I could stay alert for the drive home. When I woke up, I quickly left. It was four a.m.

On another occasion, he offered the favor of arranging for me to sleep at his friend's home during a weekend retreat, so as to save hotel costs. I figured he owed me a favor, as he had not even offered gas money for the drive home I had provided the month before. The friend was female and she had a female roommate. The arrangement included my being able to stay at the house to work on my book until the afternoon retreat activities began. I felt comfortable staying there, but at the last minute on the evening I had agreed to sleep at her home, he decided to sleep there, too. To my surprise, in the morning, I found out by talking to the roommate that the hostess had already left for her workday, and that the roommate was leaving, as well. She told me that the guy was still asleep in the other room, but that he made a regular routine of sleeping over and staying at this home during weekend retreats. I am certain he knew that the two women were planning to go to work, while I stayed alone at the house. Again, he had manipulated the situation so that we would be alone, without my consent. As soon as I realized this, and before he woke up, I packed my belongings and set out to find a suitable hotel suite. That evening, the festivities of the weekend retreat began with a large group activity. He again approached me and asked one question while we were standing right in the middle of a group of people: "So, are you afraid of men, or what?" Here was my choice point. I could have taken what he said to mean that I actually was afraid, and lost my perspective that his behavior had been manipulative and disrespectful, or I could hold fast to my position that I did not appreciate being manipulated in such a way. Never had he offered a respectful invitation to share his company, nor had he suggested that he was in the least concerned about my comfort. During this moment, I made the choice to voice my displeasure at his level disrespect, especially with his raising of such an offensive question in the middle of a crowd! He responded by stating that I simply needed to relax because he believed that men and women should be able to be comfortable with each other and to relaxed in their process of getting to know each other. In his attempts to label me as fearful and uptight, this guy was trying to pull me into a pattern of interaction wherein I would accept disrespectful and manipulative behavior. In order to do that, I would have been required to belittle myself and more importantly, would have had to accept something I did not want! I was not interested in getting to know this man in this fashion. I had already left a marriage that involved being belittled and disrespected. I was not going to walk into another relationship that was the same! This man was inviting me to wallow in the mud of a manipulative relationship which did not take my needs, feelings or preferences into consideration.

Incidentally, he was "branded" about a month later for his inappropriate mode of operating in trying to build a relationship. I was at a singles' dinner and talking with a woman acquaintance who was sitting next to me. Her cell phone rang. It was her date, the same guy, telling her that his car got a flat tire while driving on the freeway. He asked her to come and help him. She refused. After she hung up the phone and shared with me what was happening, I told her the story of my interactions with him. Apparently, his reputation then went out on the "girl network" because shortly afterward, he moved out of state.

This example reminds me of my belief that there are only two kinds of people in this world. And if we are to live our lives in a way that is fulfilling and that creates beauty through our interactions with and service to others, we must actively choose to which group we belong. I have observed, in my work with many individuals and couples as a therapist and in my interactions with hundreds of people in my personal life, that there are those individuals who are living and feeling and interacting in a very conscious manner and there are those I refer to as the "walking dead." The walking dead are those individuals who make every effort to avoid experiencing and listening to their feelings; they are those who refuse to acknowledge (maybe, because they do not understand) that to be their true, authentic, most powerful self, they must *listen* to the insights and feedback they receive from paying attention to their feeling selves. However, in most cases, the walking dead *choose* that category of life because of fear that being alive is more painful than walking around dead inside. The opposite is, in fact, true because the walking dead battle the constant fear that something will arouse them to experience their own feelings. The underlying belief is that experiencing feelings is worse than being dead.

If you are married to someone who is emotionally or physically abusive, you may have a preference for being the walking dead because you believe that walking around dead inside is safer or easier than changing your situation. If you are married to or if you are trying to have a friendship with to someone who prefers the ranks of the walking dead, and you prefer to live, you may hear them ask in disgust: "Why can't you just be happy the way you are? Why do you always need to grow?" When you tell them about a new project or adventure you are about to try, they will respond with negative energy, discouraging you from seeking your dreams. The language of the walking dead to those who choose life is a codified language that tells you that as long as you insist on remaining emotionally alive and growing with the challenges that come with living as a feeling person, you are making them uncomfortable. Your behavior of trying to understand everything that happens within the context of your relationship and trying to have a rational, emotionally responsible response to those events will be incongruent with the pattern that would allow you to be continuously manipulated and controlled in their effort to stay comfortable. Conversations in relationships involving emotionally-dead individuals seldom focus on the accomplishment of mutual goals and on how each individual can successfully have their needs met in the relationship. In order to continue with your commitment to remaining emotionally alive, you may find it necessary to actively distance yourself from the walking dead.

It is often said that if you leave a bad relationship, chances are you will go forward to create another relationship that is equally unsatisfactory. The dating interaction I just described represented a victory for me because I had affected enough change in myself that I was too alive and awake to accept the slop hurled in my direction! I had spent many years learning to recognize and resist advances by the walking dead, who would have me wallow in the mud in order to serve their purposes in a relationship with me. When I was younger, I could not see the difference between people who were alive and those that were the walking dead. In order to begin to recognize the differences,

I had to wake up. When I woke up, I began to recognize the dynamics of constricted, restrictive relationships in my life. Anyone who has awakened to recognize the unhealthy patterns in similar relationships soon comes to understand that the other participant in the relationship must also awaken or be left behind.

It is precisely the fear of moving in either direction (toward being fully-alive and being open to making changes in service of improving a relationship, or being left behind) that immobilizes others and inspires manipulative, controlling mud slinging. This is true, whether the person you are relating with is a life partner, a friend, a family member or a co-worker. The dynamic can play out no matter what the relationship. If the other person decides to stay in the mud because it is comfortable, but they recognize that your drive for something more is valid and life-affirming, they could choose to allow you the freedom to grow and encourage you, essentially letting you go, or they can become cruel. In response to cruelty, we must recognize that the cruelty comes from a place of fear for the other person. With that recognition, it is easier to avoid feelings of shame, guilt or self-doubt in response to the relationship. If we give in to self-defeating feelings, we participate in an unconscious dance that ensures that someone else gets their needs met, at our expense. While it is acceptable to choose to meet another's needs and subjugate one's own, as a willful act of altruism, it is another thing again, to participate in manipulative games without taking personal responsibility for your own needs. One example of an awakening within the context of a constricted relationship occurred in my office. During her childhood, Jane had been discouraged from doing anything independently because her mother had a fear of being alone. Thus, any moves she had made as a child toward independence were met by intimidation on the order of "You can't do that by yourself; something bad might happen to you" or "If you make that choice, God will punish you." As a result, Jane grew up fearful of trying anything alone and married a man who continued her mother's pattern by belittling and criticizing her regarding many of her daily and career decisions. In order to make decisions more confidently and independently, Jane had to recognize that mud had been slung on her from a needy mother who feared being alone and that her cooperation in the same pattern of interaction with her spouse represented her own failure to pull herself out of unhealthy relationship patterns. Before Jane made that realization, she had complained that whenever she was alone or with supportive friends, she felt confident and clear-minded about decisions in her life, but the minute her spouse had a chance to evaluate her ideas, he would question her about her choices until she actually felt like she was crazy and doubted her reasoning abilities. Since her decisions did not meet her spouse's needs, he judged them to be selfish, unreasonable and illogical, when they were simply positive steps in the direction of personal growth for Jane. Once she learned to question the process in the relationship that gave him permission to judge her negatively, she realized that her needs were never even considered in the relationship, and her husband's criticism was meant to guarantee that his were continuously met. But, in a healthy relationship, the needs of BOTH partners must be met. Recognizing the one-way quality of the relationship and her own power to change that pattern by changing the way she interacted with herself was the beginning of real growth for Jane.

Her story leads to an important point; in order to pull yourself out of the mud in the pigpen, you have to be willing to be completely honest with yourself about your own behaviors and your situation. Not only do you have to recognize when someone is slinging mud at you, but you also have to look at how your own patterns of muddy thinking facilitate your consent for remaining "stuck" in the mud. So often, we walk around with our delusions that keep us feeling protected and safe. It is sometimes scary to live with the habit of keeping your eyes open to your surroundings and to your internal responses to what happens around you; it can also be tremendously painful to realize that your relationship might provide safety by helping you avoid the fear that comes with being alive to yourself. Coming to the realization that the comfort of your unhealthy relationship is protecting you from really experiencing your feelings and living wide awake leads to the recognition that change must occur. Change is hard and scary. But change is a necessary part of living life fully, honestly and authentically. It is important to remember during those scary moments that the fear of change is often more scary than the change itself.

Once we have decided we are ready to leave the slop, we can get out of the pig pen, but the work is just beginning; our habits can cause us to stay in the mess because we are unwilling to leave the things that are said and done in the pig pen behind. For example, how many people have you known who leave a bad relationship, and then talk about the person they were in relationship with every chance they get? Or worse yet, how many people do you know who have affected positive change in their relationship, but continue to refer to "how it used to be"? What about gossip? Is it okay to talk about someone who wanted to sling their mud on us? I would suggest that the very act of making the other person the subject of conversation is wallowing in the very mud we are trying to escape! In addition, carrying a grudge toward an erring parent does nothing to move us toward healing. It keeps us stuck in the mud: feeling resentful for being dependent on a parent who made mistakes. The resentment lives on, even though we are no longer a dependent child. Deciding to stop interacting with someone by refusing their phone calls or ending visits does not mean the patterns have ended, especially with family members. If you have made a "break" from a relationship because it feels unhealthy, but still interact with that person on a daily basis in your own psyche, you are still in the mud! If you have done the work of helping a relationship to change for the better, but you constantly remind your relationship partner of how much better things are now, you are still in the mud! Interact with your own feelings and be curious and inquisitive about what is keeping you stuck until you find a pattern or way of thinking that is open to change. If you are in a bad relationship, the problem isn't the other person, it's you! What is keeping you stuck there? What do you need to think or say to yourself to make a change? When you continuously place blame for your personal unhappiness within a relationship onto your partner, you are committed to the pigpen. Investing so much energy in a pigpen keeps us in bondage to it, even if there is no literal mud on our faces; we are not free to look around and see all of the opportunities for positive self-expression that surround us. So once you are out of the mud, stay out! Cease participation in those interactions. Evaluate your thoughts and feelings related to those behaviors and choose your behaviors based on reasoning and self-control. The things we do based on our *feelings* (principally, feelings of guilt, fear or self-doubt) will inevitably land us back in the mire!

In fact, one of the principal ways we, as women, find ourselves stuck in the mud is through the experience of guilt. We don't need help from anyone else to be really good at guilt-inspired behaviors. We do it all by ourselves as well as in response to our relationships. To overcome it, we must understand the difference between appropriate and inappropriate guilt. Appropriate guilt represents those feelings we have when we recognize we have done something wrong. Guilt is the driving force toward reform. We *should* feel guilty if we intentionally harm or cheat another person. Inappropriate guilt usually comes from those shoulds we learned in childhood. For example, I might have felt guilt about not giving a ride home to the manipulative guy discussed earlier because "nice people help others out when they need help." Or, Jane might feel guilt about using part of her salary to provide self-nurturing when she goes to get a massage because she did it independently, without consulting her husband first. If I had refused to give the guy a ride home, it would not have made me a "bad" person. I would have been smart! And Jane's massage would not have made her selfish. Instead, it would help her to re-build emotional and physical reserves in order to maintain a healthy balance in life. Guilt feelings from similar events in your life are most likely tied into archaic beliefs that warrant excavation.

To explore the impact of guilt on your actions, ask yourself some questions. Can you do something nice for yourself, like get a pedicure or a massage and enjoy the experience without worry that you should be doing something else instead of enjoying some time alone? Do you feel bad about not being "nice enough" if you say "no" to someone? Do you take personal blame for things your children do that are less than admirable? Do you believe that everything your child does reflects upon the kind of mother you are? (For example, if my child is hurting, cheating, not thriving, etc. it is *my* fault for not being a "good enough" mom). Do you believe you are not acceptable to God? Do you believe that past mistakes continue to taint you even though you no longer make those same mistakes? Did someone else do something to you for which you accept the blame? (This question applies to almost anyone who has experienced childhood trauma; someone else caused the harm, but the victim carries the blame. If someone did something to you that hurt while you were a child, your guilt feelings are definitely an inappropriate response and you should seek professional help to overcome these feelings if you cannot reason through the guilt and rid yourself of self-blame.)

It is impossible to pull ourselves out until we are completely aware. We cannot recognize the pigpen until we know all of its components. In essence, we can never pull ourselves out of the mud until we have all of the mud out of our system. To do that, we need to recognize it. We need to be awake to all of the realities in our lives, no matter how painful they may be. In our interactions with others and with ourselves, we must remain painstakingly aware of the things we say to ourselves. Once we have identified that some of the things we say to ourselves are out of place, we must take action to confront those negative beliefs directly.

The ultimate question is this: what kind of a pig are you?

So, What Are You Going To Do About It?

By this time in your reading, you have likely identified patterns of muddy thinking and ways you have been wallowing in the mire within your relationships with others and with yourself. Now that you know what those feelings and inappropriate beliefs are, it is time to begin making change.

Your Assignment:

Write down what you have observed about yourself so far. I also recommend carrying a small purse-sized journal, so you can record muddy thinking and muddy interactions as they occur. Fresh mud is so much easier to describe than mud that happened two or three days ago! After you have recorded some examples, take each problematic belief and evaluate it using your grown-up reasoning. Can you recognize where that belief comes from? Is it still valid today? If you have had an emotional response to something and your response seems out of proportion to the actual event, there is something old playing in your emotions. Most of the time, such difficult feelings are not connected to current events. So, with each feeling and belief you have recorded, begin to explore: where did that feeling or belief originally begin for you? Write it down. If it was valid during your childhood, but does not make sense today, give yourself permission to abandon that way of thinking every time it arises. This is personal activism toward releasing yourself from mud that was created before you had the power to decide the direction of your own life! Give yourself permission! Do it!

CHAPTER 5

DO NOT THROW YOURSELF
IN FOR A $2 TOY!!

Value Yourself & Others Will Value You

Although it is valuable to provide assistance to others and to conscientiously provide willing sacrifices of our time and energy for the good of others, sometimes we engage in self-sacrificial behaviors that provide little value to others, at great cost to ourselves. Thoughtless self-sacrifice is yet another way to keep ourselves stuck. Let me provide an example.

In Chapter Three, I discussed the Lake Mead vacation I took with my extended family. We towed the two jet skis we took on that trip behind the houseboat, and as we searched for a suitable camping shore, one of them began taking on water. My sister saw it first. "The jet ski is sinking!" I went to help, and soon my brother was there, pulling on the tow rope to make it shorter with the belief that with a shorter rope, the jet ski would not be able to sink. Almost immediately, it was apparent that it was taking on so much water that someone needed to get out in the lake and bail the water out of it. My brother quickly put on his life jacket, jumped out, and swam to the craft. Water had impregnated the engine chamber, so it had to be opened to get the water out. During the process of getting to the engine chamber, he had to remove the seat cover, which contained a hidden cargo compartment sheltering a group of children's plastic toys. As soon as the compartment was opened, the toys began to float away. Someone said, "The toys are floating away."

Without a moment's thought, I said, "I'll get them" and with reckless abandon, I threw myself into the water. Never mind that I was wearing a sundress and not a bathing suit! I did not care about what I was wearing; I did not want the children to miss out on the fun they could have with those toys! I was also overly-confident about the fact that I am a very strong swimmer. (I had been swimming over a mile several times per week.) My mind held a singular focus of rescuing the toys, and I quickly swam to them and gathered them.

But, at the moment I leapt into the water, I had not formulated a plan beyond the rescue of the toys. So there I was: each hand full of plastic children's sand toys. Victory! I stayed there in the water for a moment, both hands out of the water holding the toys, as though I were a water polo player on the ready to defend my team. That's okay, I thought. I am good at treading water, and such a strong swimmer! I expected to be able to get back to the houseboat fairly easily even though my hands were full, albeit a bit more slowly than usual, due to minimal use of my hands. Then, I looked up toward the houseboat. Before I threw myself into the water, I had not taken into consideration the strong current or the wind that blew the houseboat as though it were a giant sail. Now, as I assessed the current and the wind, I realized that I was in trouble. Still, I continued gripping the toys in each hand, elbows bent at a 90 degree angle, as though contact with the water would have melted them. I never let go of the toys. I knew I could not get back to the houseboat – toys or not. Still, I never let go of the toys. I stayed where I was, treading water and calling out, "I need some help, here!" Luckily for me, there was in our company a maintenance team from the bay who had arrived to work on one of the engines of the houseboat. As he shook his head, apparently oblivious to the importance of the mission that took me into the water, the team leader said to his partner "Go get that woman out of the water." And, so I was rescued. But not without those $2 toys!

What is the moral of the story? I answer this question with a question. Did you notice that my brother took the time to put on a life vest before he jumped in to rescue the jet ski, but I did not, even though the treasure I was rescuing had far less value than my own life? He recognized that it was important to protect himself, even if it meant that the jet ski would have sunk completely! How often do we throw ourselves into deep water for a cause that is less important than the preservation of our own lives or well-being? How often do we allow guilt to prevent us from saying "no" when that would actually be the best answer? At the end of the day, when we have no more strength to swim, who will be there to pull us from the current if we have not taken personal safety into consideration before jumping in? It is so important for us to choose opportunities for giving to others while at the same time remaining aware of our own energy levels and turning our attention toward our own well-being before we reach the point of diminishing returns. It is quite possible that, had those toys been allowed to simply float away, no child would have missed them during our trip! And, had that work crew from the bay not come on scene when they did, I might have really been in trouble. It was a fact my family jokingly ribbed me about since I had risked myself and jumped into the water without bathing suit or life jacket to rescue inexpensive toys that the children may or may not have played with.

A similar situation occurred recently while I was talking with a female friend of mine who felt responsible for someone else's well-being. The person my friend greatly cared for had a habit of throwing herself into waters that were deep (figuratively speaking) and characterized by currents, which were stronger than her ability to swim. The details of the situation are not important because this example can apply to any situation. My friend may have been concerned about someone who seemed unable to budget her income to the point that she was always looking to others to assist her in covering the costs of basic survival. She might have been worried about her alcoholic sister, believing that she could provide help she was unqualified to give. She could have been concerned about changing the behaviors of a wayward child. What matters is that my friend was in "rescue mode;" making an effort to prevent her loved one from learning from the consequences of their own actions.

In talking to my friend, I was stunned by the strength of her feelings of guilt. Nothing I could say seemed to relieve the guilt that encouraged her to throw herself in the water, even though her own strength was not stronger than that of the person whom she wanted to rescue. Her strength and energy were being taken from her own self-care and from the responsibilities she held with her spouse and children because of her excessive concern. In my struggle to assist her in relinquishing responsibility for her loved one, I found a story that resonated for her and allowed her to regain a measure of self-preservation in spite of the struggle she witnessed. It was the story of a lifeguard.

In my training as a lifeguard many years ago, I learned a principle of life-saving that is essential for every rescuer. When a lifeguard witnesses someone drowning, a strategy for self-preservation must be in place, or there is great potential for both the life of the rescuer and the life of the victim to be lost due to drowning. A lifeguard must swim toward the drowning person while keeping her face out of water in order to keep visual contact with the drowning person at all times. Then, when the lifeguard is just outside of the reach of the drowning person, she must dive under the water and come up behind the distressed person, so that the victim cannot see her. With this plan, the lifeguard can seize the distressed person from behind, take control of the panicking person, and swim both to safety. Without such a plan, the ill-fated lifeguard will swim right into the arms of a panicked person whose only motivation is to grab onto any resource that can preserve life. To save herself, the panicked person pushes the lifeguard under water, in a blind effort to buoy herself up, not realizing that the lifeguard will drown while being used as a life preserver. When the lifeguard drowns, the victim no longer has a resource for staying afloat, quickly becomes exhausted, and drowns. By using a surprise attack from behind, the lifeguard is simultaneously ensuring self-preservation and the successful rescue of another person. Like the lifeguard, we must be wise in our efforts to help others. We must each be as aware that our efforts might exhaust both the helper and the person needing assistance to the point that harm, rather than good, is affected in the rescue efforts.

During the course of living, each of us witnesses situations involving other people struggling to avoid personal consequences. (This is frequently the *modus operandi* of the "walking dead" I described in the last chapter.) Or we witness the struggle to negotiate difficult situations that come as consequences of living during difficult socio-economic times. When we see panic and distress, a natural inclination is to ease the suffering we see. After all, we have been socialized to provide comfort and soothing, and women have a natural inclination toward easing the suffering of others. But when we are interacting with panicked people who are disconnected from themselves to the extent that their suffering is self-imposed, we must be very careful. Such individuals can have the tremendous power to pull us down with them. We must recognize those situations where our assistance will either hurt us or make no difference in the life of the person we are attempting to assist.

The most simplistic example I can provide to offer insight into this dynamic relates to how we interact with the beggar we see on the street. I frequently offer money with the awareness that such an offering does nothing to ease long-term suffering. It does not provide an answer to how the beggar will obtain food or addictive substances to relieve pain in the next day or the next week. It is only a temporary solution. It makes a difference in the moment, and when I hand over the cash I am aware that I am not providing a permanent solution. But, imagine that we decide, from our desire to provide a more permanent solution, to befriend a homeless, alcoholic man. In her desires to rescue such a man, a woman I know embarked on just such an endeavor. As their friendship developed and while she was attempting to assist him in improving his life, they decided to marry. After several years of tireless efforts on her part to reform this man and teach him how to negotiate the world without addiction, she finally recognized the toll her selfless attention toward him was having on her personal well-being. She had completely given up her sense of self to the idea that her value was derived from his ability to live sober and to become successfully employed. She gave every effort she had to assist him; and he was still an alcoholic. When she realized that she had sacrificed self-respect, health and happiness for a man who appeared quite content to remain alcoholic, she walked away from the marriage with the awareness that he would probably return to his homeless status, very saddened by his unrelenting alcohol addiction. She had finally realized that her efforts to lift him required her to absolutely abandon herself. Once she realized this, she was empowered to begin a new life of providing the caring to herself that she had hoped he would provide after he became sober and successful. As with each of us, she needed to realize that no self-sacrifice is worth it if the sacrifice has no beneficial effect on the person for whom the sacrifice is being made.

My belief is that if we are not careful, each of us has the potential of living a similar story, although perhaps on a smaller scale and with different particulars. When we care about other people, we must carefully balance between how much help we have the strength to give, we must evaluate how much of our help is actually helpful, and we must keep one eye constant on our own mental, emotional and physical reserves. Very importantly, we must not make someone else's well-being a cause that is more important to us than it is to them. Remember the lifeguard; none of us can pull herself or anyone else to safety until and unless she has the strength to save herself. Nurturing to self must come first. Then, from a place of health and strength, we can give much more effectively and find so much more satisfaction in being able to give without becoming completely exhausted.

Before going on, it is important to discuss the topic of self-nurturing. Many women do not know what self-nurturing means, nor do they know how to accomplish it. This is probably true for you if you are reading this book. It is helpful to think of your reservoirs of giving as being contained in a cup. Every time you give, some of the contents of the cup are emptied out. In order to keep giving, the cup must be refilled. How to refill the cup depends upon the personal history and preferences of each woman. But, almost without exception, refill is represented by those things we do not "have to" do, but rather those things we enjoy. For some women, if an activity does not directly relate to the feeding of her family, the happiness of her spouse or the promotion of her career, for example, the activity is deemed worthless. For these women, a continuous giving from a cup that is not continuously refilled results in their cups resembling a sieve more than a cup! No matter what these women do, they constantly feel exhausted and depleted. The exhaustion and depletion lead to feelings of depression or anger. Then, they wonder why they are doing so poorly, when everyone else in their lives seems to be doing so well (thanks to them!).

When I encounter women in this state, one of the first tasks I assign them involves getting them to come up with a list of self-nurturing activities. No one else can fill your reserves as well as you can, because you are the one most closely aware of and responsible for your personal needs. Some examples of self-nurturing activities include:

1) Playing an instrument or your favorite music

2) A day at the spa

3) Playing with your pet

4) Going for a walk

5) Devotional activities

6) Reading purely for entertainment

7) Going out with girlfriends

8) Getting a manicure/pedicure

9) Taking a dance class

10) Taking a nap

11) Taking a "me" day off work

This list is intentionally not exhaustive, because what nurtures one woman will not be nurturing to someone else. When working with a woman to help her identify a list of nurturing behaviors, I ask about those things she never seems to have time to do for herself, or those things she would like to do, but does not give herself permission to do because of finances or because someone else might think she is selfish. Those are the very activities that fill up the reserves from which we give to others. The secret to success in self-nurturing activities is that the more we give to others, the more we must care for ourselves.

So, What Are You Going To Do About It?

What situations do you have in your life that represent giving more than you should because the recipient of your energies is less committed to saving themselves than you are? With whom are you drowning in your attempts to provide rescue? (One Notable Exception: When you give more energy than you receive in return during parenting efforts of minor children, your efforts are being well-spent.)

Your Assignment

Journal about that relationship. Include your thoughts about how rescuing a person who does not make an effort to preserve themselves makes you feel safe, competent, in-control, loved or some other way. Whom are you really helping, if anyone at all?

Now, write a list of at least 3 activities you can do for yourself to help you soothe yourself instead of attempting rescue efforts that are doomed to failure (or, at least, wasted energy!). While trying to come up with these ideas, try to imagine what might feel "like a hug" to you. What activity would renew your energy and strength—an activity that you usually don't give yourself permission to do because it seems extravagant or selfish? Start the list of self-nurturing activities today. Continue to add to your list as you go about your daily activities and realize other things you could do to replenish your reserves.

The <u>key to success</u> with these activities is to do them often enough to replenish you during those times when you are feeling spent. Then, when you are feeling better, do these activities often enough to prevent your reserves from getting dangerously low.

Another note: Sometimes, a woman's reserves get so low that no amount of self-nurturing behaviors are successful in correcting a downward spiral into depression. When this is true, consult your physician to rule out any physical cause of depression and consider medication as a tool to help replenish reserves until your program of self-care is sufficient to create and maintain a positive state of being.

CHAPTER 6
THE MOVING OF THE SOILS

Your Feelings Are Your Friends – Pay Attention To Them

In this chapter, we will explore the concept that in order to be fully emotionally awake and effective in our lives, we must be fully aware of our feelings and capable of dealing with them effectively. Without that capability, the negative interactions we have with ourselves described in Chapter Three will continue to dominate and influence our actions in such a way as to promote relationships that are unfulfilling or abusive in nature. A universal experience of childhood and growing to adulthood involves some degree of avoiding feelings because sometimes feelings hurt and in most families, we were not taught how to deal with painful feelings directly. So, each of us, to some degree or another, has developed strategies for avoiding difficult or painful feelings. This is the foundation for all compulsive or addictive behavior. Whether the compulsion involves overeating, spending money beyond what is budgeted, engaging in indiscriminate sex, screaming and yelling at loved ones, using drugs or alcohol, staying in an unhealthy relationship, or any other behavior that we do in spite of our better judgment, the process of using compulsion to avoid feelings is the same.

Only a few differences exist among people who use compulsive behaviors to avoid feelings. The first difference has to do with which addictive or compulsive behavior the person favors as a tool to avoid feelings. The other difference is that each person's experience of which feelings are difficult and which feelings are not will vary. For a woman who was the victim of abusive relationships during childhood and adolescence, for example, happiness may be a difficult emotion. Because she was seldom happy during her formative years, she developed the belief that she does not deserve happiness. Therefore, any time life threatens to produce a happy experience, this woman might sabotage herself in order to avoid the discomfort that accompanies happiness. To avoid confronting her discomfort about the possibility of having a happy life, this woman soothes herself, for example, by standing up a date because the considerate, polite man who exhibits behaviors that are potentially quite loving is "too nice" for her. She dismisses him as "too nice" when it would be a better choice for her to confront her own fears about being loved in a way that does not cause pain. Instead, she stays in an abusive relationship because she believes the misery she lives in within the context of abuse is all she deserves and all she could ever find.

For another woman, compulsive behaviors serve her efforts to avoid feelings of inadequacy because during childhood she was criticized frequently. For this woman, trying new things may be difficult, and she may resort to compulsive behaviors rather than consider the possibility that if she tries something she has not done before, she might not be immediately and effortlessly successful. So, although she has a natural talent for art, she struggles a great deal with assignments in the painting class she enrolls in at the community college. Each time she finishes a painting, it clearly demonstrates her gifts. But the process of completing every painting involves seemingly endless bouts of compulsive overeating and self-induced vomiting. As she paints, she "hears" the criticisms in her head that were recorded there during her formative years and those criticisms cause her to feel insecure. She responds to the feelings of self-doubt with automatic self-defeating behaviors. This cycle might actually cause her to drop the class and decide she cannot paint, even though she is gifted.

The problem with avoiding feelings is that when we habitually avoid feelings, we run the risk of conditioning ourselves to the point where we end up feeling nothing at all. Many times, a feeling of "numbness" or "emptiness" is directly related to a long-term pattern of avoiding painful feelings. Because it is difficult to filter through our feelings and feel only those feelings that are non-threatening to us, we eventually simply shut all feelings down. Pretty soon, the moment a feeling begins to move into our awareness, our defensive system that protects us from feeling pain kicks into gear and we are into our compulsive behavior as an attempt to avoid the feelings. Often, this occurs before we have even had the chance to become aware that a feeling was surfacing.

I compare this process to the moving of the soils in a garden. When my daughter was young, I used to watch children's programming with her. I was impressed with one educational clip that illustrated the process of the sprouting and growth of a seed to the maturity of a plant. The clip consisted of a series of time-elapsed photos that began with a photograph of rich soil. Through the course of the next several photos, the soil remained unchanged as the sun was shown going up and down to represent the passing of several days. As the days passed, the photos showed the soil beginning to move, ever so slightly, over a single point in the photo. Then, the soil moved aside as the very tip of a sprout broke through. The plant was beginning to grow, and the remaining photos showed the completion of the process until the plant was mature and produced a flower, opening toward the sun. The film clip ended after less than one minute.

Our feelings are often like those time elapsed pictures. The sprouting plant represents feelings coming to the surface and the moving soil provides the cue to our defensive system that something is about to push into our awareness. When that soil just begins to move, compulsive behavior begins before the feeling even has a chance to come into conscious awareness. The compulsive behavior can be compared to placing a box over the plant which prevents the sunlight from reaching the plant, eventually smothering the plant until it no longer strives to reach for the sunlight – just as the compulsive behavior prevents the feeling from reaching conscious awareness. The more we have practiced avoiding our feelings, the more quickly our defensive system protects us from conscious awareness of them. This process is so far outside of conscious awareness that frequently, someone seeking to overcome compulsive behavior balks at the idea that in order to overcome the behavior, awareness of feelings is a prerequisite. "How I eat has nothing to do with how I feel! I just like food too much and when I overeat, I'm not upset. I eat when I'm happy!" comes a frequent protest after I have introduced the idea of moving soils. To overcome compulsive behavior, it would be so much easier to find a "magic" strategy that promises success by following a series of carved-out steps. But, the truth is that each of us has developed our compulsions in response to different circumstances. In order to overcome them, a type of emotional detective work is required to decipher the idiosyncrasies of each individual's unique process.

This detective work is performed by becoming more acutely "tuned in" to self, in much the same way as is required to be able to identify the muddy patterns of thinking discussed in Chapter Two. But, there are fundamental differences between thoughts and feelings and each have an equally different method of identification. To identify patterns of muddy thinking, one must become aware of thoughts that occur outside of conscious awareness. To become aware of feelings, one must pay attention to the location in one's body where feelings are experienced. To better understand the differences between thoughts and feelings, let us start with a basic understanding of the nature of feelings. A question I often ask people is: "What are you feeling?" Although there is really only one category of answers to that question, sometimes people confuse feelings with thoughts. So I might ask about a person's feelings and they will respond with something like: "I feel that my spouse does not like me." I respond with: "OK, so now you have told me that you *think* your spouse does not like you, but tell me what you *feel*." With that question, I might expect a response like: "I feel abandoned by my spouse." That would be a plausible *feeling*, which coincides with a *belief* (or thought) that one is unloved.

The differences between thoughts and feelings are subtle, but very distinctive. One difference is that thoughts are expressed in a form of a sentence. This is a statement of thought: "I think summer rain storms are wonderful." Most of the time, when we begin our statement of feeling by saying "I feel that . . . . " the statement is actually about thoughts instead of feelings. The word "that" signals the introduction of a thought or idea. By contrast, feelings can be stated in one or two words. For example, "I feel sad." An entire feeling can be captured in a single word. Because it is so easy to confuse feelings and thoughts, I have included a list of feeling words in the appendix of this book.

The second difference between thoughts and feelings is that feelings are accompanied by *physical sensation* in the body. To understand this, try the following experiment: close your eyes and scan your body for sensation. Keep your eyes closed until you are aware of sensations that occur somewhere in your stomach or chest. You may feel shaky, a feeling of tightness, butterflies, warmth or cold. Whatever sensations you feel, pay attention to them. Listen carefully for the information the sensations give you about yourself. Then, assign a feeling word from the list in the appendix to the sensations you are experiencing. Were you able to feel something? Sometimes, a person follows my instructions to experiment in this way and says: "I don't feel anything." You may have become very, very good at keeping your feeling shut down with many years of practice. However, pushing feelings out of your conscious awareness was a willful practice, although it might not seem to have been so. Therefore, if you have been able to control feelings by *choosing* to keep them shut down, you can also *choose to feel*. Keep trying. Think of the last time you felt very angry, sad, happy or excited. How did you know you were feeling those emotions? You experienced strong sensations in your body that you interpreted as a feeling. Keep practicing this exercise on a daily basis until you are able to recognize the physical sensations you experience and can connect the physical sensations with feelings.

Sometimes, when I assign this exercise, the question is asked: "Why is it important for me to do this?" The answer is that our feelings provide us with a feedback system to assist us in maintaining emotional, spiritual and physical balance. Without that balance, healthy relationships with self and with others are impossible. Let me provide you with a simplistic example of how our feelings work to help us maintain balance. Imagine that you are out for a walk, and you turn the corner and come face-to-face with a large, angry dog. The dog sees you and begins to snarl and growl at you. What do you feel? Fear! The fear will motivate you to take action to protect yourself and to get away from the dog safely. In a similar way, feelings of discomfort can signal us to avoid interpersonal situations that are not healthy or to take action toward positive change in those uncomfortable situations. Uncomfortable feelings can also provide a signal indicating that we need to work on our own self-talk in order to create a safer, more nurturing internal environment, and a more nurturing relationship with ourselves.

While becoming reacquainted with feelings, it is a common experience to become anxious or fearful. Trauma during childhood, like physical or sexual abuse, or traumatic experiences during adulthood, like sexual assault, very naturally lead a woman to the practice of keeping feelings outside of conscious awareness as a matter of basic survival. It is counterproductive to become overwhelmed by feelings during the times when we are supposed to be focusing on daily responsibilities. However, if traumatic experiences and the emotions associated with them are ignored, unexpressed feelings are stored as energy in the body until the time comes when they can be released. Consequently, an invitation to feel your feelings may feel like an invitation to take a trip on the ill-fated Titanic. The longer you have stored feelings without expressing them, and the more extreme the feelings you have suppressed, the more intimidating it will be when you consider allowing yourself to feel these stored up emotions. This is the reason women often fear re-visiting the feelings connected with childhood trauma. Inviting yourself to become aware of your feelings means that old feelings connected with the trauma will likely surface, like the opening of a time capsule. This idea brings anxiety because feelings that have been stored for a long time become a very powerful force, and when feelings related to the trauma return, they feel just as current and intense as though the trauma were happening for the very first time.

This is why the force of some compulsive behaviors is so strong and why anxiety can be so debilitating as to prevent you from taking a step forward in your life away from compulsive behaviors. But there is a significant difference between who you are now and who you were when you were traumatized; when the trauma occurred you were a child, and the abusive behavior posed a real threat to your survival from which you had no hope of escape. In that circumstance, it was as essential to avoid your feelings in order to survive as it would have been for Holocaust prisoners during World War II to ignore extreme hunger and pain so as not to sink into absolute despair rather than focusing on survival. Still, today is different. You are an adult now. Although you might be in an emotionally abusive or violent relationship today, you have many more resources available to you that will allow you to change your situation. Those resources were not available to you as a dependent child. Those resources include friends, family and transportation. You can read books like this one. You have the power of adult reason.

If you are in an adult relationship involving violence, escaping can be a very treacherous undertaking and should be accomplished with support. Call a counseling center in your area and ask about contacting a domestic violence shelter. There, they house women and children who are escaping violence in anonymous housing, which violent offenders cannot locate. Most of them provide supportive counseling about ending the cycle of violence and assistance to help women prepare for employment. You can also contact The National Domestic Violence Hotline by calling 1-800-799-SAFE (7233) for anonymous and confidential information, help with crisis intervention, safety planning, and referrals in your area. To obtain more information about the National Domestic Violence Hotline, look them up on the internet at www.ndvh.org. Just be aware that if you are using the internet to explore the possibility of escaping a violent relationship, you should use a computer away from your home. It is safest to access a computer at work, at the library, or at a friend's house, so the perpetrator of violence cannot find what you have been researching by looking up the search history.

Even if you are in the most extreme of situations that involves violence, it is essential that you begin to become aware of your feelings or you will stay in that situation indefinitely, passing the cycle of violence on to your children. The tendency to numb feelings associated with regular victimization is partly responsible for the reality that it takes a woman, on average, five to seven attempts to leave a violent relationship before she is able to leave and never return to the abusive relationship again. Becoming aware of and responsible for your own feelings is an essential part of getting out of an abusive situation and the only thing that can prevent you from developing a new relationship with another violent person.

Often, women who find themselves in abusive relationships during adulthood are not even aware that they are not in contact with their feelings, since they have usually coped by distancing themselves from their feelings for such a long time. One of the hallmarks of emotional shut-down is the absence of crying, although you may be experiencing a great deal of emotional or physical pain. You may believe crying is a sign of weakness. The opposite is, in fact, true. To be able to cry is a sign of strength, indicating that you are strong enough to face feelings and to allow your physiology to release the pressure of the stored-up emotional energy you have been stowing away. Crying is a much more effective method of permanently releasing energy and relieving old emotional pain than screaming is. It is a common experience that we can only hold feelings in for so long, then when we finally explode and scream and yell, the pressure is only temporarily relieved. Unfortunately, this method of emotional release does not address the root cause of the screaming and yelling.

To heal, it is essential to witness the harm that has been done to your childhood self and to provide your childhood self with an empathetic response to what you witness. This means you must pay attention to your feelings while you re-visit memories that are painful. If that experience encourages tears, cry! Allow yourself the luxury of letting tears fall that you were too afraid to let go of while you were being hurt. Think of it as a gift you are offering to your child self. Now, you have the potential to be a nurturing, protective parent toward your child within. Think of it this way. If you saw a child (perhaps your own son or daughter) that had been hurt, what would you do? Would you wrap that child up in your arms and soothe them, letting them cry if they needed to, until they felt better? Of course, that nurturing response would be what you would offer such a child; so why not offer the same compassion to the child inside of you, who perhaps never has experienced permission to cry?

Of course, you fear that if you allow yourself to cry, you will never be able to stop. Except in the case of major depression, where there is a need for medication to manage body chemistry responsible for feelings of wellness, this is simply not true. There is a kind of crying that is very vigorous and powerful. It overcomes your entire body and seems to come from deep inside. That kind of crying is sometimes necessary to let off pressure caused by old, deep pain. The truth is that your body cannot sustain the kind of energy required by vigorous, powerful emotional release for an extended period of time. What happens is that you will cry vigorously for several minutes, and then your body will relax and you will feel relieved. When I have cried like that, it has typically taken about 10 minutes, and then I was able to rest in a state of calm and quiet.

When my youngest child was about six years old, I was still in a hurtful marriage that had the effect of re-creating childhood hurts I had experienced. The situation was difficult enough that I frequently had to cry. One morning, I was crying very energetically (which cannot be accomplished quietly) while lying in my bed. My daughter came to my room to ask me if I was okay. I told her that I was okay, but that I simply needed to cry and gave her instructions to get into the shower, as it was a school day. She took her shower, and by the time she was finished, my sobs had left me quiet and relaxed. My daughter came out of the shower and saw that I had finished crying and asked me if I was okay again. I explained that I was okay and that sometimes crying really does help you feel better when you are feeling sad. Some time later, she had enjoyed an afternoon visit with a friend, but was extremely sad to see the play day end. After her friend's mother came and took her friend home, my daughter told me that she needed to cry and proceeded to climb up into my lap and sob loudly for about six minutes. I held her and just told her that it was okay for her to cry while I rubbed her back. Then, when she had finished crying, she hopped down from my lap and said: "I'm going to go play, now!" That was the end of it. In that activity, my daughter prevented herself from storing up a catalog of hurt feelings about separating from friends. Crying provided her a natural and very effective way of dealing with her sadness.

Of course, simply by providing a discussion about crying, I am not suggesting that in order to come into conscious contact with your feelings and deal with them effectively you must sob. But, it is not an uncommon experience to cry as a result of coming back into contact with feelings. Once you have pulled yourself out of the mud, there will be less of a need to cry. You will feel less pressure in your physiology and have no need to suppress feelings or tears.

The good news about crying is that it offers some relief from the feelings it expresses. The same is true for the expression of other feelings. When we experience them and talk about them, they become less powerful over us. We become able to choose our actions based on reason rather than compulsively acting in behaviors we would rather avoid, but that are irresistibly driven by emotion. Instead of being acted upon, being actively aware of and responsible for experiencing your feelings allows you to be proactive about situations that occur in your life. It is the difference between being a victim of circumstances and being able to command situations in order to meet your goals.

Similar to the concern that once you begin to cry, you will not be able to stop is the worry that once you come into contact with your feelings, you will become overwhelmed and not be able to function in your daily responsibilities. This may be true, but you must remember that you have been in the practice of shutting your feelings down for a long time. Once you have allowed yourself to feel, you can take a break from difficult feelings whenever you need to. This is a healthy coping skill that each of us uses from time to time. Diversionary vacations serve this purpose. The key idea is that when you do take a break, you do it consciously, with healthy diversionary activities (like taking a walk, taking a nap, or going to a movie with a friend) rather than participating in compulsive or addictive behavior.

In order to maintain good emotional health, we must come into contact with our feelings and be prepared to evaluate how to use the information we gain from them to determine how to interact with ourselves and with others and how to get our needs met. Although it is a bit of a scary experience to deal with feelings at first, your feelings will become a powerful ally toward your well-being. Remember, that the fear that often comes when we contemplate dealing directly with our feelings is usually worse than dealing with feelings directly. Respond to your feelings that may frighten you with the awareness that the fear cannot hurt you, but ignoring and hiding from your feelings can harm you in many different ways.

One of the ways ignoring your feelings can hurt you is by keeping you stuck in situations or relationships that are not good for you; keeping you stuck in the mud. When we consider the last chapter and recognizing the pig pen, then explore how paying attention to feelings leads to the ability to take action to leave negative situations, we can take an example from Wilbur the pig protagonist in E.B. White's book, *Charlotte's Web*. One afternoon, when Wilbur has the chance to escape to freedom, he illustrates the point that sometimes, although we recognize that being stuck in the pigpen limits our opportunities, we may choose not to get ourselves out of the mud. On one particular day, Wilbur finds himself bored and lonely on Zuckerman's farm. Wilbur's thoughts about his unhappiness are interrupted by goose. The goose is standing just outside of Wilbur's pen, and draws Wilbur's attention to the fact that there is a board loose in the pen that is keeping him captive at the farm. Goose encourages Wilbur to push through the board and run free. Wilbur does push his way out of the pen and, once he is free, all of the farm animals became excited. Even though each of them is held captive, they recognized that there is freedom, something they all desire, outside of the boundaries of their captivity. Soon, Mr. Zuckerman and his farm assistant are focusing on the task of returning Wilbur to his pen, and the other animals are decidedly on Wilbur's side. They cheer for Wilbur. They coach Wilbur in which direction he should run. They inspire Wilbur to summon his courage and strength to discover the possibilities beyond the boundaries of the farm. But, Mr. Zuckerman realizes that the comforts of what is known to Wilbur will be effective in returning him safely to his pen. Although the animals are challenging Wilbur to reach beyond the boundaries of captivity in favor of freedom, Mr. Zuckerman lures Wilbur back to the pen by inviting him to feast on a big bucket of slop. Wilbur chooses the comfort and security of what was known to him over the possibilities of what could have been found in a field of luscious roots. In some ways, we are like Wilbur after he escapes the safety of the pen. He probably feels some fear when he is being pursued by the farmer in a different way than he had experienced before he had ever attempted an escape. When he sees the aggressive efforts of the farmer to trap him, he probably chooses to accept the slop because it is more comfortable than being chased and yelled at.

In a similar way, experiencing your own feelings will confront you with the challenge of sometimes taking a stand that changes the way you interact with others and how you allow others to treat you. But, to do that, you will have to summon the courage to venture beyond the limits of your normal behavior. Will you reach beyond what you know, even though it might bring fear and unknown adventures, or will you stay comfortably where you are even though your potential is stunted when you choose to stay comfortable? Will you take the challenge to learn to listen to and nurture yourself? Can you summon the courage to become your own best advocate? My favorite definition of courage is: feeling fear while confronting and overcoming the challenge that inspires the fear. Face the fear and overcome. Courage is essential because it is the cost of freedom. Essentially, the most important thing is to learn to nurture yourself, to give to yourself, and to hear your own truth about whether you belong in the pigpen or whether you are radiant and marvelous and beautiful. Remember, to advocate for yourself in this way may mean that you have to take a stand against destructive voices from your past and others who are comfortable when you accept less for yourself than what you deserve.

So, What Are You Going To Do About It?

Think now about the possibility that you could summon your courage enough to really learn to hear your own voice, to acknowledge your feelings and to honor yourself.

Your Assignment

What fears would you have to overcome to be able to do that? Whom would you displease by honoring your feelings? Get writing! Remember, the act of listening to your feelings and honoring them IS NOT an active act of rebellion against anyone. To reclaim yourself in this way represents a return of loyalty to your own foundation. From that place, you can give with wisdom. If anyone suggests that your feelings and responses to them are invalid, think of what you would need to do to honor your own voice. Nobody outside of you has veto power over your feelings – whether that person is present in your memory as in childhood trauma or whether they are a real-life, present-day person who would rather you ignore what you feel in order to serve their purposes. Journal about the fear you experience when you think of honoring your own feelings. Now, give yourself permission to recognize and honor your feelings as valid. Practice awareness of your feelings every day. Your feelings do not hurt anyone and they can only assist you.

CHAPTER 7

WAIT!! WHO ARE YOU TO DEFINE ME??

You Know You Best – YOU Decide Who You Are

A natural outgrowth of the process of learning to deal with your feelings and of resisting the pressure of allowing your actions to be directed by others is the re-definition of self. The process of defining ourselves based on our experiences with the world begins relatively early in life. I have discussed some of this process during my discussion of the differences between how girls and boys are socialized in Chapter Two. My daughter who aspired to be a bull rider provided an illustration of this point. Her desire to be a bull rider did not subside. She continued to talk about riding a bull for weeks. She is a very active child who enjoys strenuous physical activities. For example, at three years of age, she tirelessly persisted in learning how to do the hand-over-hand horizontal ladder monkey bars. During her learning process, she fell, cried angrily and got right back up and tried again until she could traverse the vertical ladder as well as the older children. She has always been focused on the activities other children were capable of doing, and when she saw a fun activity that challenged her, she relentlessly pursued it until she mastered the new skill. As a result, she mastered skills usually accomplished by children at an older age. For example, at the age of four, she was riding her bike without training wheels. It seemed she was on a quest to conquer every fun activity she witnessed. As she became aware of fun activities which required more challenge, she began to notice bull riding, jumping bicycles over makeshift ramps, rough games of tag and vigorous sports activities. As she observed these things, she noticed that it was boys who were doing these fun things. So, shortly after her announcement that she could ride a bull, she proclaimed "I want to be a boy." As I questioned her about why she wanted to be a boy, she clarified "because boys get to do all of the fun things." Somehow, her observation that boys were doing the things that looked fun caused her to conclude that those activities were reserved only for boys. Her dismay at not being a boy, and thus being locked out of the fun in life, provided me with a teaching opportunity that I hoped would arise again and again during her growing up years. My desire was and is that she will recognize that although society can provide definitions to her of what girls can and cannot do, she has the final decision about whether or not she will subscribe to those definitions. With that philosophy in mind, I shared with her that although it looks like boys are the ones who get to have the fun, there are some really fun girls who like doing those things, too. I explained to her that she was one of those fun girls and that she did not have to be a boy to participate. Then, to reiterate what I wanted her to learn, she and I made several trips to the vacant lot where some boys had built bike ramps out of dirt so we could play on our bikes the way the boys did. During the process of re-defining the kind of girl she was allowed to be, we developed the concept that she was buff, strong and brave. Afterward, whenever she approached a challenge and wished to overcome apprehensive feelings, she used the mantra we had developed together: "I'm a buff baby." As a result of this experience, her self-esteem was boosted and she no longer wished to be a boy.

Just as my child observed that boys are the ones who have fun, girls and women (and boys and men) develop patterns of belief based on observations of how the world works around them. As I grew up, I developed the belief that "women are stupid" as a part of a similar process. I had noticed that boys had an easier time in math classes than girls, and I had observed my father taking a strong, protective role with my mother, who was then allowed to be feminine and soft. They made decisions together, but I was unaware of their process of talking things over and deciding together, as they did that behind closed doors. So I watched my parents' relationship and took further confirmation of my developing belief. The ranks of society and religion also confirmed my observation, since women are not typically found in positions involving making decisions for "the masses." My conclusion from all of these observations was that "men are smart and women are stupid." The interesting part of that belief was that I had externalized it to include "women" but never to include myself. Imagine my dismay on the day I realized that I fit into that category as well! Yikes! I did not make this realization until after I had completed my Associates and Bachelor's degrees and was half way through my Master's degree. Then, I realized that the reason I had graduated at the top of every class, had been inducted into Phi Beta Kappa, and had earned straight A's in all except two of my classes was from a subconscious drive to prove that I was not stupid! I would have had so much less anxiety and would have actually enjoyed my education had I not been so driven to disprove that belief! It wasn't until the last few quarters of my Master's program that I realized I had been really working hard to prove I was not stupid. The funny thing is that no one believed I was stupid, except me! So, during the last six months of my education, I realized that I could give about thirty percent *less* effort toward my studies, still achieve academically and enjoy the process instead of being endlessly driven to "prove" myself.

When I look back on that time, however, I recall there was certain evidence in my life that still indicated that I was stupid. These were the forces that helped to keep my motivation to prove otherwise alive. Principally, I remember that my marriage relationship supported the belief that "women are stupid," even though my husband would have denied that he preferred a "stupid" woman. In fact, he took great pride in how "book smart" I was, but criticized and put me down if I drew a conclusion that he was uncomfortable with or that did not serve his needs. He also had a subtle way of using his sense of humor to suggest negative things about me. But when I suggested that his humor was hurtful, he insisted that he was "only kidding" and gruffly dismissed my feedback. He dismissed my discomfort with the way he treated me by telling me that there was something wrong with me. In his view, I was overly emotional and sensitive. For a while, I accepted these negative definitions he placed upon me, but it was impossible to do so once I began paying attention to my feelings and recognizing that I was the only person who could improve the way I felt. Soon, I began to reject his ideas about me that were negative and deprecating and I began to verbally challenge him when he suggested that I was inferior. Unfortunately, my process of rejecting negative implications about who I am ultimately resulted in the final dissolution of the marriage. But an exploration of unraveling my belief that women are stupid illustrates the process of how setting out to prove ourselves can keep us stuck in negative situations.

At the time that I met and married my first husband, the belief that "women are stupid" was firmly rooted as part of my unexamined belief system. As a part of the coupling process, I naturally attracted men who shared that belief. So regardless of which of those men I had chosen to marry, the undercurrent of the relationship would have suggested I was inferior in some way. Like self-fulfilling prophecies, it is a common habit to cast ourselves into roles that personify unexamined beliefs in our choice of whom we will couple with. Once we have done that, our quest becomes proving the unexamined belief wrong in order to prove that we are loveable. During my first marriage, I had succeeded at winning my husband's approval in the sense that he bragged to others about how good I was at everything I did. He told others that I was a "good wife," a "good cook" and a "good student." But, in private, his criticism discounted anything he had said to others to shed positive light in my direction. To prove myself loveable, I strived harder to be what he told me in private about what he thought I should be. But, as any effort to please another person in order to get their approval and develop self-respect is misguided, I was unable to succeed in winning his unconditional approval. That had a lot more to do with who he was than about the quality of person I was.

To extricate myself, it was necessary to first *hear* myself. The entire process of pulling myself out of the mud of that relationship began with my realization that if I wanted to by happy, I needed to stop treating myself poorly. As soon as I stopped treating myself poorly, I naturally disallowed any poor treatment from others, including my spouse. It is not necessary, however, that in order to change the way we see and treat ourselves, we must sever relationships. Sometimes, the people with whom we are relating will recognize, honor and support our efforts to feel better about ourselves. When we are surrounded by supportive people, we can discuss the changes that are required as a result in our shifting perspectives about ourselves. Those discussions will lead to shifts that can accommodate our changes. But each woman who is unhappy with herself and/or in her relationships must begin by examining her attitudes and beliefs about herself. Ask yourself: "What am I looking for in my relationship?" Are you trying to prove something within the context of your relationship that you would be better suited to address within yourself? Let's explore this concept further.

As I have previously stated in Chapter Two, it is a common experience for women to allow their roles to define who they are. So, when a woman gets married, she often defines herself as "Mrs. Soandso" or "Soandso's wife." It is as if the act of getting married somehow enlarges her. While it is true that the process of marriage is intended to initiate growth, the *act of getting married* represents a joining of two individuals rather than a fusion of selves. The difference between joining and fusion is neglected while preparing for marriage and must be explored in order to encourage healthy individuality within the context of the merging of two souls. Marriage symbolizes the uniting of two individuals in purpose as each partner commits to the common goals they identify as a couple. Discussions regarding bringing children into the union and managing finances together represent the process of developing and working toward these common goals. Traditionally, marriage has indicated the initiation of "becoming one" in the physical sense, as well. The process of uniting in purpose and joining physically and financially does require abandoning selfishness toward a larger focus on the prosperity of the marriage, but *it does not require the abandonment of self.* In fact, the abandonment of self will undermine the health of the marriage relationship.

A woman who abandons herself in order to fulfill her new role as wife and mother focuses all of her attention toward the good of the union and the good of the children. In that process, she neglects to recognize that her own needs will be neglected by others if she sets the example of neglecting them herself. And in doing that, she exhausts herself and becomes resentful when her spouse does not attend to her needs as they arise – without communicating to him what her needs are. Instead of taking care of ourselves, we begin to look to our spouse to take care of the needs that we are personally responsible for. The logic behind the expectation that our personal needs will be met without communicating them comes from the reality that women generally give everything we know how to give in order to intuitively and successfully meet the needs of our spouses and children, so we expect that they will also intuitively and successfully meet our needs. The problem is that this process does not work through osmosis, although we expect it to! Women also frequently make the mistake of giving everything, to the point of exhaustion, with the expectation that the re-fueling will come from the marriage relationship in a way similar to how an intuitive and conscientious mother attends to a small child's needs through a process of divination. I am aware that I am repeating myself, here. But, the concept is so essential, yet difficult for many women to recognize in their own relationship patterns.

There has to be a growing-up process. To continue to look to your spouse to automatically know what you need and to help you feel better without taking initiative yourself to see to your own well-being is to remain a child. Grown-up women take personal responsibility for how well or ill they feel. Do you feel physically unwell? It is your responsibility to fuel your body with healthful foods and to get enough regular exercise and adequate rest. If you do not take personal responsibility for those things, you are remaining a child by looking for sympathy and assistance with things that are within your control. It is adult behavior to get someone to look after the children while you take a nap. It is adult behavior to make sure that you get good nutrition, just like your family does. To complain about being tired and to wait for your husband to get the hint that you need some more rest is childlike behavior. Frequently, it does not work. Have you been making poor relationship choices in your personal life and on the job? Do you constantly complain about it to whomever will listen instead of taking corrective action and directly addressing the relationship problems with the parties who have direct interest in the difficulties? Complaining is what children do. Take the problem directly to the source and begin looking for mutually acceptable solutions. That's grown-up behavior.

Taking personal responsibility for our own needs extends to how we respond to being labeled by others and by what labels we place upon ourselves. Think of the roles you fulfill in your life: what do you call yourself? Are you "wife," "mother," "daughter," "friend?" If you identify yourself this way, do you also assign yourself other labels like: "creative person," "innovative problem-solver," "effective time-manager," "expressive dancer," "enthusiastic athlete" or "imaginative crafter?" Do you regularly devote some of your time and energy to personal pursuits that fulfill and interest you? How do you define yourself outside of the roles you perform? Those activities that you pursue *outside* of your responsibilities are the very activities that provide the wellsprings of self-soothing and well-being. Inevitably, marriages end, children grow up, parents die and friends separate. When these things happen, how much of who you are will end with the relationship? The answer to this question indicates the extent of your need to establish your own identity and to take personal responsibility for your own emotional needs. When you are hurting, afraid or sad, do you have the resources within yourself to find soothing? If you cannot cope without leaning on another person, you would do well to evaluate how grown up you really feel. If you are able to soothe yourself, you will also be able to resist the negative influences imposed by derogatory labels others would place upon you.

Unfortunately, I witnessed a very sad and ironic example of labeling in a negative way when a certain man came to my home to visit with his wife. He began stating to everyone in the room that he admired my posture and the grace with which I carried myself. I thought it to be a generous compliment, but before I had a chance to respond, he turned to his wife and asked her: "Why can't you be more like her?" It was such an offensive comment and a useless compliment because it was used to belittle instead of to build up. I felt that the way I carried myself betrayed her. I felt sad and offended. I could see the hurt in her eyes and commented that it would be of little value for her to be like me, because she had beauty of her own that he should appreciate. Unfortunately, my suggestion fell flat as he was oblivious to how insensitive his comment was. My only hope was that she could hear my suggestion and recognize that her value should not be defined by cruel and insensitive statements made by her spouse. This provides an example of how he labeled her. He did not call her clumsy or stooped directly, but I am sure his comments led her to understand that "more like her" indicated "not acceptable enough" to him. If she was listening to and honoring herself, she would have responded by recognizing her own hurt and making some statement which withdrew permission from him to criticize her in such a manner, especially in public. Had I been in her place, I probably would have said something like: "Excuse me? You are right, she is beautiful, but who says I need to be like her? My value and beauty are unique. If I were like her, my own qualities would be diminished because they would no longer be mine." Hopefully, she defended herself once they left our home. If she had, she would have been taking personal responsibility for her wellness and validating her personhood.

Instead, many of us look to others to find out if we are "good enough." By doing that, we never develop the personal strength to stand on our own and validate ourselves enough to create balance and happiness in our lives. I believe that our search to find validation outside ourselves is responsible for much of the rivalry that also exists between women. If we could value ourselves without comparing ourselves to each other, I think we would be much more capable of developing supportive, loving friendships that are devoid of jealously and competition. This concept was recently re-iterated in my mind as I began taking an intermediate belly dance class. I had been studying using video tapes at home and had begun to feel less challenged in my beginning belly dance class. So, with the teacher's permission, I advanced to the next level. From the moment I began preparing for the evening's class, I was inundated with self-doubt. Was I too inexperienced to join the more advanced women? Would they think me presumptive to be joining their group? Would I be criticized for wearing lovely costumes to class, since I did not know how to dance as well as they did? I worked very hard while getting ready for class not to allow those thoughts to drive me away from attending. But, when I got to class, the self-doubting conversations in my head continued. I noticed other women's moves looked more controlled and precise than my moves. I felt judged, although no one indicated that I did not belong. I felt critical of my body. In short, by the time the class was over, I felt miserable, although I did not show my feelings outwardly.

Sometimes feelings like the ones I've described here will drive a woman to project the criticism she feels about herself toward other women. Sometimes, feelings like these will inspire her to withdraw. In fact, feelings such as these had been the reason that I had stopped attending dance class twice before, taking breaks of a few months long each time. This time, I was determined to stay, knowing that the feelings had to be worked through in order for me to triumph and to validate myself with such an affirming form of dance. While driving home from class, I stewed in my negative feelings long enough to identify what my thought patterns had been during class. Then, I sought encouragement and direction from my teacher about the struggles I was having during class. Her insight was indispensable. I had been struggling during class because of my focus on others, my need for validation from sources outside myself and because I had abandoned my practice of self-validation during class. I had become so caught up in what I guessed others might have been thinking of me that I had stopped thinking about what I was impressed with about myself! I had allowed that focus to prevent me from enjoying what I was doing and from concentrating on improving my experience and enjoyment of the dance. While it is true that during the beginning class, I had encountered moments of becoming mesmerized by the movements in my own body, in the intermediate class, I was so focused on what other women were doing and my own imaginations of what they thought that I was not focused on my dance at all. The result was a miserable experience! Thankfully, I learned that I needed to focus on my own practice and forget what other women are thinking and doing in the class. I think this is a lesson applicable to many more situations than a dance class. This mistake that prevented me from enjoying the dance class is frightfully common for many women. We get so caught up in what we fear others are thinking about us that we forget to enjoy our own journey. The solution is to focus away from other people and away from concerns about what they may think. Instead, we must each focus on our own journey, on our own enjoyment, on our own improvement and on our own process. We need to tweak that old adage, "Stop and smell the roses." We need to smell the roses in our own gardens instead of comparing our garden to those of other women and finding that theirs smell better than ours. We need to "Stop and smell *our own* roses!"

At this point, I would like to refer back to the way we develop as human beings. One concept in human development is the concept of "mirroring." Essentially, when we were children, we looked into our mother's faces[1] for feedback about how "good" or "bad" we were. If our mothers looked at us in loving, accepting ways, we were and are much more likely to be loving and accepting of ourselves. However, if we perceived our mother as critical or rejecting, we were and are much more likely to be critical and rejecting of ourselves. This is the seedbed of self-criticism learned in childhood. Because the habit of self-criticism and self-rejection is so painful, we tend to look to others for approval since we are unable to provide it to ourselves. The result is that we continuously look into others' faces (most often seeing criticism because that is what we are used to seeing) and continuing the cycle of self-rejection. To break this cycle, we must take back the process of validation. That is, we must learn to appreciate ourselves and to cease allowing deprecation to be validated by our attention simply because we haven't yet realized that seeking approval outside of ourselves is a left-over habit from childhood.

For example, how do you respond if you do not get consistent praise from your spouse about the "job" you are doing as wife and/or mother? If you are unhappy because other people are not recognizing your contribution, let me ask you this question: "What makes you believe that the other person is a better judge of the quality of your contribution than you are?" We should not be taking care of our responsibilities with an eye toward the kind of pats on the head that we got when our parent posted our art work on the refrigerator during grade school. If we are, we are giving personal responsibility for validation of our self over to someone else. Take it back! Pat yourself on the back for things you do well. If you need improvement in some areas, do what you need to do to improve. Begin to evaluate your own progress instead of looking to someone else to provide that evaluation for you. Remember, if you are looking for some form of "good girl" from someone else, you are also unwittingly giving them power to label you as "bad." Why not take personal responsibility for recognizing your own positive qualities? This way, you can judge when you need improvement and, in doing so, prevent unwelcome criticism that only serves to undermine you as a person.

The distinct advantage to only applying labels to yourself that are positive and self-imposed is that it frees you up to take care of yourself. No longer are you waiting to be "good enough" in order to spend some time focusing on self-care. Taking care of yourself becomes a matter of routine maintenance rather than a treat reserved for when the children are grown up, when world hunger is relieved, when your spouse finally retires or just before you die. I make these statements not to be facetious, but to illustrate the point that if we wait to take care of ourselves until after everything else that needs doing is completed, the self-care will never happen. One of my favorite poems was written by

Carol Lynn Pearson and is available in her collection of poems entitled *Beginnings and Beyond* (Cedar Fort Press). It illustrates this point beautifully. Take it in.

MILLIE'S MOTHER'S RED DRESS

It hung there in the closet
While she was dying, Mother's red dress,
Like a gash in the row
Of old, dark clothes
She had worn away her life in,

They called me home
And I knew when I saw her
She wasn't going to last.

When I saw the dress, I said
"Why Mother – how beautiful!
I've never seen it on you."
"I've never worn it," she slowly said.
"Sit down, Millie – I'd like to undo
A lesson or two before I go, if I can."

I sat by her bed
And she sighed a bigger breath
Than I thought she could hold.
"Now that I'll soon be gone,
I see some things.

Oh, I taught you good – but I taught you wrong."
"What do you mean Mother?"
"Well – I always thought
That a good woman never takes her turn,

That she's just for doing for someone else.
Do here, do there, always keep
Everybody else's wants tended and make sure
Yours are at the bottom of the heap."
"Maybe someday you'll get to them.
But of course you never do.
My life was like that – doing for your dad,
Doing for the boys, for your sisters, for you."
"You did – everything a mother could."
"Oh, Millie, Millie, it was not good –
For you – for him. Don't you see?
I did you the worst of wrongs.
"I asked for nothing – for me!"
"Your father in the other room,
All stirred up and staring at the walls –
When the doctor told him, he took
It bad – came to my bed and all but shook
The life right out of me, 'You can't die,
Do you hear? What'll become of me?'
'What'll become of me?'
It'll be hard, all right when I go.
He can't even find the frying pan, you know."
"And you children –
I was a free ride for everybody, everywhere.
I was the first one up and the last one down
Seven days out of the week.
I always took the toast that got burned,
And the very smallest piece of pie."
"I look at how some of your brothers
Treat their wives now
And it makes me sick, 'cause it was me

That taught it to them. And they learned,
They learned that a woman doesn't
Even exist except to give.
Why, every single penny that I could save
Went for your clothes, or your books
Even when it wasn't necessary.

Can't even remember once when I took
Myself downtown to buy something beautiful —
For me."
"Except last year when I got that red dress,
I found I had twenty dollars
That wasn't especially spoken for.
I was on my way to pay extra on the washer.
But somehow – I came home with this big box.
Your father really gave it to me then
'Where you going to wear a thing like that to –
Some opera or something?'
And he was right, I guess.
I've never, except in the store
Put on that dress."

"Oh Millie — I always thought if you take
Nothing for yourself in this world
You'd have it all in the next – somehow
I don't believe that anymore.
I think the Lord wants us to have something –
Here – and now."
And, I'm telling you, Millie, if some miracle
Could get me off this bed, you could look
For a different mother, 'cause I would be one.
Oh, I passed up my turn so long

I would hardly know how to take it.
But I'd learn, Millie.
I would learn!"

It hung there in the closet
While she was dying, Mother's red dress,
Like a gash in the row
Of old, dark clothes
She had worn away her life in,
Her last words to me were these:
"Do me the honor, Millie,
Of not following in my footsteps,
Promise me that."
I promised.

She caught her breath
Then Mother took her turn
In death.

As Carol Lynn Pearson illustrates in this poem, we hurt more than ourselves when we abandon ourselves by giving past the point of exhaustion or by accepting labels that do not serve to build and strengthen us as individuals.

Millie's Mother imagines that she would have left a much different legacy had she learned to be selfish sometimes. In fact, something curious happens when we expect only to receive the best treatment for ourselves, whether it is in how we treat ourselves or in how we accept others' treatment of us. If we treat ourselves with the utmost respect, we will then give from a place of self-respect. We will respect others from a place of strength. We will teach by our example that to love is not to diminish the self, but to expand our capacities to love based on a foundation of strength, respect and love. It is a spiritual principle. We cannot give what we do not have.

Necessarily then, if we accept only what is positive for ourselves and practice self-preservation at those times when our reserves are running low, our daughters will learn to do the same. Our sons will seek relationships with self-assured, confident, loving women. We will pass on a generational pattern of respectful individuals. So, let us focus on passing down positive habits of self-respect. Let us begin from this point forward to describe our children as focused, confident and beautiful rather than strong-willed, difficult or self-centered. Let us teach our children to view their characteristics in terms of how those characteristics can be channeled toward their goals and toward improvement of their societies of friends. To do this, we must identify all that is good in us and in them. When will we begin to say to ourselves that "I am beautiful, strong, competent, and capable?" Can we each challenge ourselves to do so? It does not break any real rules or harm anyone to say those things. It can only engender strength in us and in those with whom we associate. I know that such questions might be dismissed with wishful statements like: "Yeah, that would be nice" or "That would be so hard to do." My suggestion is that the only thing that makes it difficult is that perhaps negativity toward ourselves is a well-practiced habit. We can change our habits! Of course we can!

Let me share part of my journey toward reversing the habit of being so negative toward myself in hopes that it can give you courage and inspiration. I have already stated that I could not accept negative treatment and comments toward me within my marriage once I recognized that those comments were not worthy of nor characteristic of me. As my story continues, I found myself remarried just thirteen months after leaving a spiritually and emotionally oppressive marriage. This time, I am married to a fabulous, loving, supportive man. (The difference between my first husband and second husband had been no accident. I had completed about 15 months of intensive weekly personal psychotherapy while pulling myself out of the first marriage and before I met my current husband. It is true that if we leave a marriage without doing any work to change ourselves, we will end up in an identical relationship, even though the new partner has a different face. God also played a huge role in my second marriage being as supportive and loving as it is – He is the one who got me to stop running from a very wonderful man!.) During the brief period that I was single, I talked with friends about the kind of man I envisioned in my future. I wanted someone who would adore me. A man who could not get enough of me. A man who could not keep his hands off of me! A man who would cherish and value my spirituality and my intellect. These were not simple things and I intuitively knew that these were things I *needed* to heal and to become my best self. I wanted and needed romantic, fairy-tale love.

By talking about it and dreaming about it, I sent my wishes out to the universe, and the universe responded! I got just the man of my dreams! But, then I had a new problem. The mud of the past that had kept my feet stuck in a dead marriage for almost fourteen years now threatened to suck me back down because my internal reality did not match my external reality. What does that mean?

Well! One of the realities of the fourteen years I spent in a dead marriage was that I needed and used food to keep myself dead enough to stay. I was miserable, but one of the hallmarks of using food to cope is that as long as you are chewing, you can numb yourself. It was a strategy that worked well. It helped me tolerate the misery. Once I was re-married, I reveled in the thrill of being loved unconditionally, so I did not worry about what I ate. And, we enjoyed eating together, so although I had lost about 10 pounds of my "bad marriage weight" during the year I was single, I gained it back along with 25 *more* pounds during the first eight months of marriage to my new husband! I complained to my doctor. He explained that for unknown reasons, people who are happily married gain weight. He told me that research supported the phenomenon and that if my husband was not complaining that I should not worry about it. Hogwash! Unknown reason?! The so-called unknown reason was that I was eating too much! And, I was not going to accept that I had to be fat if I was happily married!

I decided that I needed a weight loss program. I knew it was the next step in the healing process that began when I left the first marriage. I wanted to improve my physical health and feelings of self-confidence, but mostly, I wanted to develop a healthy relationship with food. I carefully considered it and joined a popular program. I enjoyed success right away. I lost 20 pounds in the first two months. Then, it started . . . . sabotage, sabotage, sabotage! I lost a pound, and then gained it back. I would stay on my program, then "decide" that I *wanted* to be fat and eat off the program. For FIVE MONTHS, I sabotaged myself and stayed at about 20 pounds of weight loss. Just five pounds more than I weighed on the day I married Mister Wonderful!

Why could I not get past that point? What was wrong with me? Here I was, a licensed Marriage and Family Therapist, who helps other people figure things out, and I could not get it! Not only was I frustrated with my lack of weight progress, but I was feeling intense feelings of disappointment. For about three weeks, I was walking around and saying, "I have everything in my life to make me happy. I have a fabulous husband who loves me. I have a satisfying career. My finances are getting into order. My relationships with my family have been repaired. I have an active spiritual life. I am working on several books. My creativity is flowing. But I am so *unhappy!*" I could not figure out why. It did not make any sense. Finally, at the end of the three weeks, I called my therapist and went in for a "tune up" session.

I described this unrealistic and uncharacteristic unhappiness. I was shaking and crying, filled with so much anxiety that the room felt cold to me, although it was not. My therapist asked me what I was most fearful of. I knew that answer right away: it was that my husband would stop loving me. My therapist reassured me that my fear was not going to become a reality, based on his knowledge of my husband. Then, he helped me to calm myself down by walking me through a guided meditation focused on diaphragmatic breathing. He reminded me that I was the one who calmed myself with the breathing technique, encouraged me to use diaphragmatic breathing regularly and sent me on my way.

The next day, I awoke in the morning to get ready for work with the previous evening's session still on my mind. I was convinced that the anxiety was simply more of the mud I needed to wash off and determined that I would pay attention to my breathing on that day. From the time I got up until I was out of the shower and dressed, I must have caught myself holding my breath six times. I have come to realize that when I hold my breath, it is my attempt to disallow feelings from surfacing to my awareness. (I have also observed many women who do the very same thing!) So I focused on consistent breathing, staying aware and in the moment, staying calm.

Once I was dressed, an amazing thing happened. I had dressed myself and was standing in front of my bathroom mirror while I placed a choker necklace around my neck. Breathing. Just as I clasped the choker, I looked up at my neck, in the mirror. Then, quite without the permission of my internal critical sensor, I observed: "Wow. I am really beautiful." Not an affirmation. Simply an observation.

Then, as if the critic that lives inside my head had been put to sleep by the breathing – just long enough for something positive to happen - and abruptly jarred from sleep with the observation, a flood of memories returned. They were memories of critical moments in time from which I drew the conclusion that I could not be beautiful and be loved at the same time. Some of those memories developed in the same way that Cinderella might have learned not to allow the love of her Prince into her heart because of what she had learned in her family. She was beautiful. Her stepsisters were not. They were jealous and cruel to her. Had Cinderella drawn the conclusion that the sisters were cruel *because* they were less beautiful than she was, she could easily have drawn the inference that she was not loved because she was beautiful.

The interesting reality here is that the stepsisters did not even need to be ugly. As long as Cinderella had *the perception* that she was more beautiful than they and that this was the reason they were cruel, the groundwork was set for creating the belief that being loved and being beautiful were incompatible. It suffices to say here that I had neither a cruel stepmother nor ugly stepsisters. I had and still have a very loving, very human family. I also had experiences outside of my family with friends and associates while growing up that reinforced my thinking regarding being beautiful instead of being loved. The belief represents coping strategies, developed in childhood and adolescence that are not necessarily based in objective reality. I use this illustration simply to outline the dynamics that were present to develop this pattern of thinking.

Another reality that developed this pattern of thinking for me relates to my experiences as a teenager of having no romantic interests. When I would talk with my father about my disappointment at seldom being approached to be asked to dance or about how infrequently I dated, his explanation was that I was too pretty. He stated that because I was so pretty, boys were intimidated about asking me to dance or asking me out. Gee! How do I fix that? I wondered. A definite conclusion was being drawn that being pretty was incompatible with positive relationships with the opposite sex.

When the flood of memories came back to me, I was able to recognize that they were relics of the past. My visit with the therapist had awakened the sleeping giant of beliefs that were causing my current discomfort in my marriage. Now, I was aware of what those beliefs and thus, I was responsible for changing them. Whatever the experiences were that convinced me that I was not allowed to be beautiful as well as loved; I recognized *in that moment* that the conclusion represented distorted childhood thinking. It was certainly *not* based on the reality of the present! I *am* loved. I am loved by a marvelous husband. I am loved by a family who has never abandoned me, even when I behaved in unloving ways. I am loved by God. Yes. The conclusion that I cannot be beautiful *and* loved was in error. I recognized it right then and there. And I gave myself absolute permission to be beautiful! I am loved. Why not be beautiful, too?!

How did I give myself permission? Well, I started by saying it out loud. Over and over again, I repeated: "I give myself absolute permission to be beautiful!" Nobody else needed to give me that permission but myself. It became my mantra. Each time I repeated it, I felt more courage and strength. I realized that the way I viewed myself made every difference. Now that I had absolute permission to be beautiful, I naturally looked for ways to express it in the way I presented myself. I recognized that by wearing clothing that fit too loosely and neglecting my appearance just a little bit, I had been downplaying my beauty in order to be loved. Now that I had given myself permission, I began going to my closet every morning and looking for something that I felt beautiful in. Although I usually wore make-up before this revelation, I began applying it with more care and attention to enhancing my beauty. In essence, I began to embrace those habits that acknowledge and enhance me as a beautiful woman who is loved.

As I am writing this, I am aware that a focus on beauty might serve the opposite of my intentions here in that our culture focuses on a level of beauty that serves to degrade the average woman. Unfortunately, the media defines beauty only within very narrow margins – and the media and entertainment industries too often force feed us with impossible standards and calls those impossible standards a cultural definition. But, if we look at a more realistic definition of beauty, we will find much more satisfying parameters. A more realistic definition of beauty, I believe, more closely approaches what true beauty is.

The American Heritage dictionary defines beauty in the following three ways: "1. A quality that pleases or delights the senses or mind. 2. One that is beautiful. 3. An outstanding example." These definitions clearly indicate that beauty is more than visual aesthetics. What I would like to propose here is that beauty includes those qualities of personality that are pleasing to the mind because they bring about good in the world. A woman is beautiful if she is honest, true, chaste, benevolent, virtuous and if she does good whenever she sees the opportunity to do so. A beautiful woman has strength and peace in her soul based on a foundation of awareness of her inherent goodness. What does this have to do with dress size or flawless skin? Nothing!

Indeed, we can all think of a woman who is visually beautiful, but who behaves in ways that cast an unbecoming shadow on her physical beauty. In fact, that kind of person may indeed be described as ugly simply because of the way she conducts herself. At the opposite end of the spectrum, think of examples of women who may not be visually beautiful, nevertheless, we define them as beautiful. An excellent example of this is Mother Theresa, who spent her life in service to the sick and dying in the streets of Calcutta. Her mission was to assist the poorest of the poor to die with dignity. For her life's work, she was awarded the Nobel Peace Prize. Hers was a life of service, peace and love. To look at her, she was a small, wrinkled old woman. A beautiful woman. Her beauty shone from within her soul as a result of doing what she followed her destiny to do. There is inherent beauty that radiates from a woman whenever she is true to good values and centered in her awareness of herself.

Recently, I was providing some church service when I came across a remarkably beautiful young woman. She was so appealing to me that I could not help but stare at her. Upon first glance, some would say that she was terribly ugly. Although half of her face was lovely to look upon, the other half was disfigured and distorted. Her jaw on one half of her face was large and masses of tissue under the skin pulled her mouth to one side. The eye on that side of her face was similarly disproportionate, pulled down at the outside corner because of the disfigured jaw. The non-distorted side of her face held my attention because she appeared extremely peaceful and happy. Indeed, she was beautiful and dignified based on what appeared to be a solid sense of her own worth. I continued to watch as several of her associates expressed words of delight when they came into her presence and greeted her with hugs and warm conversation. She was captivating and her beauty was found in the radiance that others felt in their association with her.

Another example comes from an experience I had in the waiting room of a legal aid office. It was during a time when I was especially dissatisfied with my level of physical fitness. In the waiting area of the legal aid office, each legal aid client signed a clip board, and then sat waiting to be called from the list. As I sat there, a woman in her mid twenties entered the room. She wore a pair of dressy jeans with a black tee shirt. I recall being stunned by her beauty. The reason I felt stunned is that she did not fit into the cultural definition of beauty. Indeed, at that time in my life, I was expecting myself to fit into the cultural norms prescribing thinness as a prerequisite to beauty. But, this young woman walked into the room and challenged my thinking. Her clothing fit her snugly enough to show her figure, but not so tight as to be binding. Her jeans were probably a size 18 or 20. And she had dressed herself and attended to her hair and make-up with care. Perhaps, her beauty was in how she carried herself. She walked with confidence. She had great posture. She seemed very self-assured. It seems that if I would have had a conversation with her, she would have acknowledged her own beauty.

I learned from her and from the other women whose examples I have used that in order to embrace our own beauty, each woman must have the courage to define it for herself, then have the courage to magnify whatever aspects of self make her beautiful! Each woman must give herself <u>absolute permission</u> to be beautiful! We must begin by rejecting the definitions others place upon us. As women, we all were required to traverse the awkward and difficult stage of development known as adolescence. From that time in our lives, many of us carry around the seeds of negative self-concept. Think back to your most awkward time growing up. Were there negative definitions placed upon you? What were they? How much power do you give them to keep you feeling badly about yourself today?

When I was in middle and high school, I was called "Monkey Face," "Jolly Green Giant" and "Carpenter's Dream." I was six feet tall by the summer I turned 16 and always taller than my peers, so "Jolly Green" was an awkward adolescent attempt at humor. "Carpenter's Dream" referred to the perception that some had indicating I was as "skinny as a nail and flat as a board." I have no idea how "Monkey Face" came to be, because I was not an ugly teen. In fact, although I did not compete, I was a finalist invited to participate in the Miss National Teenager contest based on the photos I submitted. Looking back on pictures of my teenage years, I have to dismiss any perception that I was unattractive, although the unfortunate labels assigned to me by my peers had inspired insecure feelings. With that correction of my perception based on hindsight and photographs, I am led to ask the following question (and invite you to do the same):

What would it mean about me if I say that I know I am beautiful? It would mean that questions of self-worth that arose based on a faulty self-perception would not have limited my potential. I might not have hesitated to accept opportunities based on fears of being inadequate. Who loses if I am beautiful? Nobody! Does embracing my own beauty mean that I am "conceited"? Perhaps, but what does that label really mean? It means that the "conceited" person has a more positive, realistic sense of herself than those who are applying the label. (I feared that label in High School, and yet, among a group of young adults who each have different levels of developing sense of worth, being worthy of conceit may have been an admirable trait!) Perhaps, I would have claimed the privilege of marking my own path based on a solid sense of confidence. Perhaps, my confidence and self-acceptance would have forced those name-callers to assign their negative projections elsewhere. To have one more beautiful person in the world is no loss to anyone. When we see our own beauty, we are that much closer to being able to finally put to rest the shackles created by "I can't" and "I do not deserve it." We should never allow what others think or say about us to limit our belief in ourselves.

Try an experiment. Think of those qualities about yourself that you appreciate. Think of at least one. Now, close your eyes and in your mind's eye, elaborate on those positive qualities. Imagine that you became well-known among your associates for those qualities. Imagine that you give yourself permission to magnify all of your positive qualities. Would you not be able to accomplish more than you allow yourself to accomplish now? Would you have a sense of confidence that gets you over the "humps" when you encounter difficulty in accomplishing a goal?

Imagine the women I have already described in this chapter (Mother Theresa, the woman with the deformed face, the woman in the legal aid office). Had they chosen the path of self-doubt and self-criticism, would they have been capable of bringing good to the world? No! It would have caused them to be self-limiting. Yes, self-limiting. We can be as beautiful as we allow ourselves to be. If we allow our own doubts to get in the way, there will be less love, less beauty, less courage in the world.

One more idea before I close this chapter. Because I am six feet tall, I frequently receive comments from women about my height. They often envy my height and ask if they can have some of it – half in jest, but half wishing (as they tell me) that they could have more height as a weight-management strategy! Yes, they often envy that I probably can eat what I want and still have a flattering figure because I am tall. I often joke that although height may have its advantages, it also has disadvantages, such as the inability to ignore the dust that collects on top of the refrigerator because I can see it every time I go into the kitchen! I bring this idea to this discussion because it speaks to the need for each woman to embrace her own uniqueness. When I was a young woman, I often enjoyed playing basketball and flag football as part of wholesome co-ed activities. On a specific occasion, I remember being encouraged to abandon my fear and self-consciousness with the encouragement of the young men to "be the ball." The phrase meant that I should stop thinking, worrying or analyzing and be present and focused. "Be the Ball." To women, I say, "Be beautiful." You cannot be six feet tall if you are not. But, you CAN be what you are! You CAN be your best qualities. If you can be it – whatever "it" is – let go of your self-doubt and be it now!

Dare yourself to be as absolutely beautiful as you know how to be. Give yourself the courage and permission to ignore anyone who would have you be less than your very best self.

So, What Are You Going to Do About It?
Your Assignment:

In your notebook, make a list of all of the positive and negative feedback regarding your own beauty that you received during your adolescence. Next to each item on the list, write the names of the people who gave you those labels. Look back over the list . . . . Who on the list was interested in your growth and well-being? Give yourself permission to rebel against those who were not interested in your good with the labels they attributed to you. Next, make a list of your positive qualities. It is okay if you only have one or two for now. If you cannot think of any, choose something about yourself you are least critical of. Now, write an affirmation that gives you absolute permission to have that quality. Say it out loud! Celebrate it!

CHAPTER 8

NOBODY HAS TO BELIEVE YOUR DREAMS BUT YOU

How To Transform Your Dreams Into Realities

To this point in our discussion, we have explored how our childhood dreams develop, what gets in the way of our dreams, and how to identify and confront negative patterns of belief that influence our behaviors in such a way as to keep us stuck in muddy relationships with ourselves and with others. My goal in developing these ideas is to bring each reader to the position of being able to accomplish her dreams. In order to reach our dreams, we must remove everything within us that prevents us from believing our dreams are attainable, including the tendency to allow others to discourage us because they do not believe in our dreams.

The only prerequisite for attaining your dreams is that you hold on to them tightly and do not let anything dissuade you in your journey toward them. Several months after my daughter first watched the rodeo, I asked her if she was still going to ride a bull. When I asked the question, the same gleam returned to her eyes that I had seen on the first day. She responded with an emphatic "Yes!" I think if she holds on to that dream, she could very well be the first woman rodeo bull rider. We can attain our dreams, but we must really, really believe them.

My daughter is such a supportive influence toward my dreams and she supports the idea of really, really believing. Like all writers, one of my dreams is to be interviewed on the Oprah show about my book. While it may or may not happen, and my success as a writer does not hinge on that occurrence, the dream has been something that has helped to motivate me to write when writing has not been the most attractive activity I could choose. But once I shared my dream of having Oprah tell the world to read my book, my child began to ask questions that encouraged me to visualize my dream more vividly. She asked me: "Why do all of the people clap for her when she comes out?" With that question, I realized that she was visualizing my dream as if it were a certain reality. Her question encouraged me to do the same. Next, she asked: "How tall is Oprah?" Then, I began to think about how tall she is and what it will be like to walk out on stage to greet her. She continued her visualization further and declared "I want to say, 'Hi, Oprah! That's my mom!'" During conversations like these, my child takes me on a journey that encourages me to confront my own doubts and to keep the dream alive. It feeds my inspiration.

By contrast, my oldest daughter has had visions from time to time of going to dental school to become a dentist. When she shared that idea with her friends, one of them responded with "Yeah, right." To challenge the disbelief, my daughter invited her friend to make dental school her goal, as well. The response came: "I cannot go to dental school with you." I tried to encourage her to continue holding onto that dream, but the power of her friend's negative response resonated with my daughter and she decided that she was not going to go to dental school. And, in that moment I realized that if I believed in her dream and she did not, the dream had so much less power to motivate her.

The contrast between how my youngest daughter responds to my dreams and how my oldest daughter's friend responded to hers brings up the question of how we will respond to the "nay sayers" who hear our dreams and communicate their disbelief. Do we simply stop talking about our dreams? No! In order to make our dreams a reality, we must talk about them. In the process of talking about them, we come to believe them. We also attract others who will support us because they believe us when we talk about them. But there will always be those who will communicate their disbelief when we talk about what we wish to achieve. In a recent conversation, I mentioned that one of my goals was to be on Oprah. I stated the goal as a reality, almost as if it were already achieved. Someone who was standing nearby said: "Wow. That goal is aiming high." The tone of the statement indicated that he thought I was reaching for an unattainable aspiration. I turned to him and said simply, "No, it's not." I am sure my response got him thinking, because my response was just as confident as his. That conversation got me thinking about why the "nay sayers" seem compelled to rain on parades. As I thought about it, I realized that when we dare to dream and set goals meant to propel us to a better life than we or our associates are accustomed to, those dreams and goals get some people thinking something like: "Gee, I could never do that. I'm just an average person. No average person thinks like that or does those things." (What happens in their head could be even more negative if their muddy thinking habits are strong and unexamined.) Then, by comparison, they assume the same thing about us because we look like an average person to them. But, we are breaking the rules that exist in their head because we are audacious enough to display our aspirations publicly! People like this are members of what I call the Skepticism Society (SS). When we audaciously parade our dreams in front of them and dare to believe those dreams, we break article one of the SS constitution: "No person may claim to be above average nor aspire toward goals that would make them stand out from the crowd." The slightly bad news is that whenever we are bold enough to expose our dreams in public, there will always be the Skepticism Society. The fantastic news is that what goes on inside the heads of members of the SS and what comes out of their mouths regarding how achievable our dreams are has *nothing whatsoever* to do with the validity of our dream! Article two of the SS constitution: "As a card-carrying member of the esteemed Skepticism Society, each member carries an obligation to reflect his or her self-doubts and negative thinking toward any person found breaching article one." With article two, the SS is compelling its members to participate in an activity called projection; this is what happens when someone projects something they believe about themselves onto someone else. Don't accept anyone else's projection that you cannot reach what you dream of! The truth is that everyone who has boldly pursued audacious dreams until those dreams became realities had to ignore the SS! And, every time one of us becomes wildly successful, the SS shows up again! This time, they are adhering to article three of the SS constitution: "Whenever a member in good standing encounters a person who breaches article one and believes themselves to be successful, the member will strenuously seek to publicly reveal the character flaws of the person breaching article one." So, if the SS is after you, congratulate yourself because you are reaching for high-quality audacious dreams! The presence of the SS is actually evidence of astounding potential. And they will provide a never-ending witness to your astonishing success! (If they only knew how encouraging it is that their mere presence provides proof of victory! Of course, if they knew that, we might be able to convert some of them over to living joyfully. Wouldn't that be exciting?!)

So, if "nay sayers" present an obstacle to believing our dreams and we are able to let them wallow in their own disbelief without joining the SS, what other obstacles get in the way of believing our dreams until they become realities? In my mind, there are two significant possibilities outside of the complications I have already described in the first seven chapters of this book: time and fatigue.

Time! There are two ways we allow time to make us believe our dreams are out of reach. The most obvious is that we can fill our lives up and become so busy with daily routines that we never seem to get around to what is important to us. This is a condition related to not being a high enough priority in our own lives. If this is a problem for you and you still need to understand how to move yourself from the back burner to the front burner, go back to Chapter One and start reading again! (The concepts described throughout this book take time to understand and incorporate. Evidence that you have successfully mastered them comes in the forms I am describing in these last three chapters. Go back to the beginning and study and practice until you get it!) Everyone has the ability to find a few minutes to an hour or more each day to devote to her personal agenda. It really is a matter of making yourself a priority. A fabulous way to accomplish that is to make sure everyone gets to bed on time (say, 9 pm – and that includes yourself), then you can arise early for uninterrupted personal time. I typically get up at about 4am when I need focused time for myself. Of course, there will come a time when I do not have dependent children and I will have the luxury of sleeping in, and taking more time for myself. But right now, if I want to accomplish my dreams, I have to start before the sun comes up. It is really a matter of priorities. Value yourself enough to make your dreams your priority.

Now, if the SS reads this book, it is likely they will call me some kind of "women's libber" who is advocating abandoning family values and responsibilities in pursuit of selfish rewards. Au contraire! Pursuing your dreams does not have to be mutually exclusive with values that are involved in raising a family. Of course, if you leave your young children at home for a year so that you can travel Europe on foot, you have abandoned your family. But what I am talking about is achieving your dreams while you take care of your family responsibilities. And I assume that if we have families, it is part of our dream to raise confident, well-adjusted, loving, responsible, creative children. This book was written with that concept as a centerpiece, as you will see in Chapter Ten. The point I am trying to make is that as women, we have been trained to believe that we can do one or the other, but not both. That is a fallacy that keeps us from having the courage to discover our dreams. We have to stop thinking in a way that places what we want for ourselves in conflict with what we want for our families. They are not necessarily mutually exclusive choices. So, I can nurture and raise and build and strengthen my family at the same time that I can nurture my own dreams. And I do not have to give up one to do the other.

The second manner in which time is a threat to your dreams is that it keeps moving forward. Time does not stop. Whether you are closer to achieving what you dream or not does not matter to the clock! Think of it—where will you be in five years from now? What will have become of your dreams? The answer really depends upon what you do and what you believe today! The reality that time passes requires you to do something on a daily basis that contributes to the fruition of your dreams. Remember, too, that although you are doing something to move closer to your dreams every day, these things take time. Do not allow the passing of days and weeks and years to cause you to give up too early.

As I sit here today finishing my first book to be published by a New York trade publisher, I look back and think of how often over the past six years I have said: "When I get my book published." Yes, I said that for SIX years before it became a reality. In actuality, this is the second book I have finished, but it is the first one to be published. Before I found the publisher for this book, I received rejections of my first book from publishers for TWO YEARS! Six years and two books later, my dream of becoming a published author is coming to life. But what would have happened if I had quit after one year, or two, or three, or five? Or, what would have happened if the fact that I did not get my first book published right away prevented me from writing my second book? I don't even what to think of it!

But, here is what I know. I know that for six years, I spoke in positive terms about the dream I was working on. I talked about it to anyone who would listen. And I talked about it as if it were a definite reality: my book WILL get published. I said: "When my book is published" instead of "If my book gets published." There is a clear difference in the language and strength of belief in each of those statements. The first almost guaranteed eventual success because it got me ready for success. It made me keep my eyes open for opportunities, and when the opportunity presented itself, I grabbed it! In fact, my path to publishing this book didn't even follow the usual route of queries and submissions and rejections. Let me tell you what happened so I can show you how my belief in my dream resulted in my becoming a published author.

I was frustrated because of the two years of rejections of my first book, so I started doing research on the internet about marketing books and self-publishing. I found Planned Television Arts. I looked at their client list and saw: Suze Orman, Jackie Collins, Tom Brokaw, Nora Roberts, Jack Canfield, Dean Koontz, Dr. Phil and others. When I saw whose bestselling books had been represented by this company, my dream that I BELIEVED motivated me to e-mail the president of Planned Television Arts, Publicist Rick Frishman. I knew I had it in me to be a bestselling author. People simply needed to know who I was! So, I asked him about the possibility of hiring his company to market my self-published book, *Pull Yourself Out of the Mud*. He responded to my e-mail almost immediately and asked what my book was about. Two or three e-mails later, Rick connected me with David Hancock, of Morgan James Publishing in New York. One month later, I had a publishing contract! Thank you, Rick! But that publishing contract would have never come to fruition had I allowed time or frustrating events to discourage me. My *belief* had to be strong enough so that when the opportunity came to approach a major publicist, I was not intimidated.

Let me share another example of frustrating events that served as a bump in the road, but did not derail my pursuit of my dream. About three years ago, I had organized a group of professional women in the hopes of forming a supportive, creative environment that would provide the catalyst for each of us to publish a book and to develop an empire of support and empowerment for women everywhere. I was committed to raising our vision together and developing a community that would last for years to come. The first sign that my dreams weren't believable to them was that while we each talked about and began working on a book, the idea of self-publishing quickly became the order of the day. I resisted that idea and refused to accept anything less than "big time" for my ideas. Some of the women chose self-publishing, and that was okay for them. But I refused to settle for that. I refused to lower my ambition. It paid off. Yes, it took three more years, but I held on to that dream long enough to see it through. Persistence and patience are strategies that work. Unfortunately, one of the women in the group was a card-carrying member of the SS, and her efforts at upholding the SS constitution ultimately led to the complete dissolution of the group. That did not cause me to let go of my dream of building a world-wide supportive network of women reaching toward their dreams, though. But I'll get back to that in a minute.

Another example of defending my dreams against the power of the SS comes to mind. I had a friend who had provided significant assistance to me and my family while my husband was diagnosed with an aortic aneurism and a severely leaking mitral valve. His life was in danger and he needed open-heart surgery. The time from diagnosis to surgery was two months and it took my husband a year to recover completely. During that time, my friend would twirl into my house and do helpful things for me. She seemed to know what I needed even when I did not. From those experiences with her, I decided that she was a good friend. But after things got better for me and my family, my friend did not seem as able to provide support. Every time I talked to her about my dreams, she had negative comments. I once told her about my frustration that my first book had been rejected again. She asked me: "Who commissioned you to write it?" I could not believe my ears! I said, "What do you mean?" She said, "Has someone told you they would pay you to write that book?" I said, "No." Her response was, "Well, good luck with that." I hung up the phone in disbelief. I felt as if she were telling me that she believed I could not be successful in selling my book once I finished it. I decided I would talk to her about the problem (convert her from the SS and bring her online with my vision). Although I tried to tell her my perceptions, she was not open to hearing what I had to say. Unfortunately, I had to let go of that friendship because each time I had shared my dreams with her and she responded in typical SS style, I found myself doubting my dream. Dreams never flourish nor become realities in an environment of doubt. Sometimes, holding on to your dreams means being picky about whom you associate with. Do not allow a friendship with an SS member to squelch your ambitions.

The point of the stories in this chapter is to help you recognize that in order to obtain your dreams, you must: 1) *Believe* them!, 2) do something toward them every day, 3) be persistent and patient and 4) recognize the SS but don't join them!

Something magical happens between the conception of a dream and its realization, if you believe. Holding on to the dream like your life depends on it makes something tangible happen. You make something that began in your imagination develop its own life. You develop the motivation to overcome obstacles. Your confidence grows! Once your belief has grown to the point of boosting your confidence, something else happens. People begin to see something different in you. They will see you glowing. They will feel the passion that drives you toward your dream. That energy and those around you who see the passion growing in you will continue to provide you with the energy and motivation you need to move toward your dream. The universe will respond and provide you opportunities to see your dreams become realities. Yes, it is like an upward spiral. It's fun and enlivening.

Now, let me get back to telling you more about my dream for women everywhere. I believe we, as women, have spent far too much time fighting with each other and not nearly enough time building and strengthening one another. Jealousy and bickering among women only serves to blind us to our strengths and how powerful a team we could be if we simply supported each other in our ambitions. When I talk about competition among women,

I am referring to the reality that if you or I see a woman walking toward us on the sidewalk and she is wearing the same dress that we are, our first response is competitive. We think, "What the heck? That's *my* dress! Get it off!" But what would happen if when we passed on the sidewalk, we offered each other a high-five and a shout-out for mutual good taste? Let us acknowledge the beauty and the praiseworthy things we see in each other. I often complement women I see, even if I do not know the particular woman by name. Just last month, I saw a young woman with her family while I was walking with my husband. She was wearing a lovely yellow dress that looked beautiful on her. As I came near her, I said: "That is really a beautiful dress on you!" She seemed both startled and pleased by the compliment. My hope is that we can make a habit of building each other up, so much that when a woman whose name we do not know pays us a compliment, our response is not shock, but mutual accolades for being a member of a world-wide support network!

Let us look for the good in each other. We need to tell each other about the good we see. Tell your friend how thoughtful you think she is. Compliment your co-worker on how hard she works. If you admire someone, don't assume she knows how much you admire her. Tell her! If we could each develop the commitment within ourselves to pull out of the mud together, think of how powerful we will all become! I do not know who got women competing with each other, but I know that we can begin cooperating with each other simply by making that choice. Then, we can build a global network of support. We can smile at each other and look each other in the eyes rather than looking down toward the sidewalk as we approach each other. Women are not strangers! We have remarkably similar experiences. We need to share those experiences with each other and build strength together. With this in mind, I have developed a gathering place for us to meet and build and support each other. Eventually, I see us meeting several times throughout the year, in various locations, to support each others' dreams. For now, let's start here: www.GetOutoftheMud.com. Let's build support for each other. There is also a page at www.GetOutoftheMud.com where you can make your dreams public. Go to the site. Read my blog and share your thoughts and feelings about our support network. Let's share our dreams and our victories with each other. Let's start a worldwide support revolution! Let's drive the SS crazy! Together, we can do anything!

So, What Are You Going to Do About It?

I hope by now you are as excited as I am. So, I ask you again, What are your dreams? Who have you shared them with?

Your Assignment:

Start talking!!! Go to www.GetOutoftheMud.com and start believing! Make a list of the people you need to share with and share! Make a list of the SS in your life, too. Recognize who they are. Now, give yourself absolute permission to ignore them! What are you waiting for? Get going! Do something today and every day toward your dreams and you might just be surprised by how quickly your dreams become realities.

CHAPTER 9

DECIDING HOW HAPPY WE WILL BE & HOW HIGH WE CAN FLY

Decide Today To Stop Limiting Yourself

Once upon a time, there was a farmer who noticed a nest built into the hollow stump of a dead tree just outside his farm. The nest had one very large egg inside. Having studied birds his entire life, he easily recognized the egg as belonging to a couple of bald eagles. The farmer decided to watch the nest so that he could study the family cycle of the eagles he had discovered. To his dismay, an entire morning passed with no adult eagles attending to the nest. The farmer felt terribly sad and guilty, since he had heard his dogs creating quite a ruckus the night before. Based upon his knowledge of the sensitivity of eagles during their nesting period and the character of his dogs in protecting their farm and the surrounding property, the farmer deduced that the adult eagles would not come back and decided to take the egg into his care. He carefully carried it to the chicken coup and placed it in the nest of one of his hens.

The hen dutifully sat on the egg, as she did not notice the difference between this egg and her own, although the eagle egg was rather larger than the others in her nest. Soon, the egg hatched and the farmer was quite proud of himself for devising a plan to save the baby eagle. He allowed the hen to teach the eagle chicken behaviors so that it would be able to eat, and the little eagle grew. The baby eagle learned to scratch his enormous talons in the ground, seeking seeds and worms. Although it bothered the farmer to see that the eagle never seemed to look up from the ground where he foraged for food, the farmer soothed himself by planning to help the eagle learn to fly as soon as he was strong enough, about three months after it had hatched.

Unfortunately for the farmer and the eagle, the opportunity window for teaching the eagle to fly passed as the farmer became consumed with harvesting his crops in order to continue to support his family and home. Once the harvest was over, the farmer again turned his attention to the eagle. By now, the eagle had grown for six months and should have recognized his own majesty, strength and beauty. Inspired by the visions in his head of this beautiful creature soaring the sky, the farmer picked him up and thrust him toward the sky. "Fly, my majestic friend! Fly!" The bird didn't even spread his wings; instead it fell to the ground with a thud. It stood up and shook its head, then began walking around in circles, pecking at the ground. Undaunted, the farmer perched his reluctant friend atop the highest post in the chicken yard. "You must understand that you are not a chicken! You are an eagle! Fly!" The eagle just looked at him, seemingly afraid of having been placed upon such a high perch. The farmer gave him a nudge. Again, the eagle fell to the ground with a thud. The farmer feared he would injure the eagle by continuing with this process, so he gave up his efforts for the time being. He hoped the eagle would eventually look to the sky and natural eagle instincts would take over and draw the eagle heavenward.

One year passed, and then two. The farmer had tried at various times and in various ways to help the eagle recognize his destiny. But, the eagle remained an over-grown chicken for the remainder of his life. Fifteen years after the farmer rescued the eagle egg from the abandoned nest, the eagle died inside the chicken coup after a morning of pecking the earth for food. The eagle lived his entire life and died believing he was a chicken.

The original author of this story is unknown, and I have taken some liberties to craft it in a way that supports the point I want to make. I make my point with this question: Do you live your life pecking and scratching at the ground when you could be soaring through the skies as the beautiful, majestic eagle that you are? This is a similar question to the one I asked when I encouraged you to decide: "What kind of pig are you?"

You see, so many of us allow our circumstances and others' opinions of us to limit us. We do this by taking on chicken habits! We do it by proudly wearing the mud that other people are comfortable in. We might recognize the patterns, but still do nothing. Why? Because like the chicken eagle, we develop the habit of being comfortable with mediocrity. We become frozen and unable to move out of the habit of believing that our dreams are out of reach. For a long time, I thought that I *could* reach for my dreams if I wanted to, but because I had become so used to not having permission to pursue anything audacious, I did nothing. I was an eagle, but only saw myself as a chicken. It was *me* stopping me from flying because the only person who needed to believe that I was an eagle was *me*! Think of it, the eagle in the story was only a chicken based upon its experience and belief. That experience and belief had nothing whatsoever to do with its innate power and strength! An eagle with chicken habits is just an overgrown chicken!

In order to become the eagles that we are, we must figure out what the real truths about being an eagle really are. The truths of an eagle are that your wings are strong, your legs are long, your vision is keen, and your knowledge is broad because of the heights to which you fly. To be an eagle, you must face your fears and confront the chicken beliefs that you hold to be true. I have already said a lot about confronting your beliefs as I described muddy thinking patterns. Fear is an entirely different subject. As the chicken eagle proved, it is impossible to have the fears of a chicken and fly like an eagle – even if you are an eagle.

Sometimes, we avoid reaching for our dreams because we fear what will happen if we do. As I have looked closely at my fears, I have discovered several things. First, I have realized that fear is really an illusion. Secondly, I have come to understand that fear is an essential element of faith. Let me tell you a story about how I learned that fear is an illusion. It starts in my childhood, as most of our fears do. When I was about 5 years old, I lived next door to my maternal grandparents. Our back yards were separated by a chain link fence. One afternoon, my three-year-old brother and I were playing in our back yard and took notice of our grandparents' Australian Shepherd watching us play. We went over to the fence and began putting our hands through the fence and poking sticks through the fence in a way that quickly agitated the dog. I remember noticing that the dog was becoming angry, but I did not seem bothered by his anger because the fence gave me a sense of security. That is, until the dog began digging under the fence. Soon, my brother and I recognized that the dog was coming under the fence to get us. We both turned and ran. He made a bee-line for the back door of our home. I headed straight for the slide of our swing set, thinking that I would be out of the dog's reach. As soon as I got to the top of the slide and looked behind me, I saw that the dog could reach me if I stayed on the slide. So, I slid down the slide and ran for the door. I did not make it into the house. By the time my brother alerted our mother to what was happening outside, the dog had pinned me. Just outside the back door, my mother found me pinned under the dog as the dog ferociously chewed on my face and throat. My mother saw me with my head in the dog's mouth and began kicking the dog to get it off of me. Then, she rushed my brother next door to our grandparents' house and rushed me to the hospital. At the first hospital, the physicians refused to help. Instead, they referred us to a plastic surgeon, where I received 36 stitches to repair my face and throat. Thanks to the expertise of that surgeon, I have only a few minor scars. They are unnoticeable to anyone unless I point them out.

But, even though that dog left undetectable scars on my face, he left seemingly indelible scars in my heart and spirit. From that day forward, I carried a paralyzing fear of dogs. It wasn't until my early thirties that I recognized that the fear was limiting me and that I didn't have to allow it to do that. Although it had been three decades since the dog attacked me and I had grown stronger and at least three feet taller, I experienced terrible anxiety at the thought of going outside for a walk by myself. I was afraid that I would encounter a dog. The interesting part about my fear is that it did not even matter how big or small the dog was; I was afraid to meet one! Here's the funny part. One afternoon, I was walking in my neighborhood, pockets laden with rocks I had picked up along the way, just in case I bumped into a dog out for a walk. I rounded the corner and there, I saw exactly what I feared: a Chihuahua! I saw him and stopped in my tracks, immediately reaching into my pocket for a rock to throw at him in warning. I had learned that dogs can smell fear, so I tried to posture myself so that, in spite of what he smelled, I was a formidable foe. Of course, he stopped and then decided to do some posturing of his own. He barked fiercely, trying to compensate for the difference in size between me and him. If you would have been watching, you would have seen a comedic exchange, wherein neither of us dared turn away from each other as we made a large circle around each other before we could head in opposite directions. My fear and adrenalin were as if I had encountered an angry Pit Bull! I went home, pondering the scene I had just participated in.

I began to explore the validity of the fear that had gripped me so tightly that I didn't even recognize that one swift kick of that Chihuahua would have sent him careening down the block! I realized that the little dog had not actually posed any threat to me at all. I began exploring the fear more completely. I drew some conclusions. I was much bigger and posed a much greater threat toward any dog that would wish to attack me as an adult compared to my 5-year-old size. Most dogs responded in a passive way if I looked them squarely in the eyes, yelled at them and stomped my foot. Ninety percent of the dogs I was likely to stumble across did not even care about interacting with me, much less attacking me! I was attacked because I had been actively antagonizing the dog! Don't antagonize a dog and most of them will ignore you completely. Once I began exploring the fear, I was able to conquer it. I realized that the fear maintained its hold based on realities of my childhood that were no longer true. Sound familiar? Now, I frequently go out for walks and never have to fill my pockets up with rocks as a prerequisite to going outside.

The moral of the story is: Don't run away from Chihuahuas! Every fear in your life may have been based in reality on some part of your history, but since that time in your history, you have had opportunities to learn things that make those fears invalid. If not, go investigate and learn what you need to in order to quell the fear! This principle applies even if your situation is as extreme as domestic violence. You have read this far. You are educating yourself. Figure out what your resources are so that you can face your fears and change your situation for the better. (Find a counselor who can help you address your fears. A qualified counselor can assist you in safely escaping a dangerous situation.) The fear will not get better if you do nothing to stop it from taking over your life. Every time I have faced one of my fears straight on, it has evaporated as if it were a mirage in the desert. The closer you get to your fears with an attitude bent on overcoming them, the more they begin to dissipate. Try it; I am sure you will find the same to be true. It is a simple principle.

Let me provide you with another example. Recently, my family took a vacation and found a fabulous indoor pool with water slides, a kiddy pool, a tide pool, lap lanes and diving boards. My daughter wanted to learn how to jump off the high dive. She asked for my help. I decided that the best way to help her conquer the high dive was to show her that even though it is scary (I was scared, but I didn't tell her that), it could be done. Because I wanted her to jump off that board without allowing her fear to stop her, I told her that once she began climbing the ladder to the top of the platform, she should not allow herself to stop. She should just climb straight up, walk to the end of the board and step off without pausing long enough to feel afraid. "Like this," I said, as I began climbing the ladder to show her how to avoid pausing because of fear. All the way up to the top of that ladder I was thinking "I can't believe I'm doing this! It is really scary! I don't want to jump off this high dive, but I want my child to believe in her ability to do something scary without fear." Next thing I knew, I had landed safely in the water. She followed my example, and before the day was over, she had jumped off that high dive at least a dozen times. She felt the fear, but jumped off the high dive anyway. That's courage! It's not much different than the courage we use to confront any of our fears.

Another part of overcoming our fears is understanding that fear really is an essential component of faith. Without fear, we would never feel the push to exercise faith. Conversely, faith is what assists us in overcoming our fear. The American Heritage Dictionary lists faith as: "1. Confident belief or trust in a person, idea, or thing. 2. Loyalty; allegiance. 3. Secure belief in God and acceptance of God's will." According to these definitions, faith has differing applications, depending upon the belief system of the individual. Yet, faith and fear still work hand-in-hand, no matter which definition we explore. In the first definition, a confident belief must come from extricating any doubts or fears that the person, idea or thing is correct.

The journey toward confident belief requires us to explore and reject anything that goes against the belief. According to the second definition, loyalty or allegiance connotes having a choice between remaining true or abandoning ship. Loyalty to our dream means that we hold on to it – we have faith in it and take action toward it – until the dream becomes a reality. In the third definition, if we believe in God, then we also recognize that God expects us to have faith in Him. To do that, we must recognize our own fears, but set them aside and replace them with unwavering belief that God will provide for our best good. Any way we explore it, faith involves being actively engaged in identifying and confronting fear. It involves an *active* choice to move away from fear and into belief. Essentially, fear is a tool that shows us what we need to do to strengthen our faith. Once confronted, our faith (or belief in our dreams) is so much stronger. In this sense, fear can be our friend.

That may seem like a radical idea, but consider this: in order to accomplish the sort of real, lasting changes that allow us to actively reach toward our dreams, we must be willing to make sacrifices and take risks. Every sacrifice or risk is an act of faith because the sacrifice is made or the risk is taken in the *hope* of a positive outcome. The positive outcome is simply a figment of our imagination until it becomes a reality. Hope sufficient enough to take a risk or make a sacrifice represents a leap of faith!

Think of the things you have already accomplished in your life. Can you see that *each step* you made toward a goal you had not yet achieved represented taking a risk? About three years ago, my husband and I were in an intractable financial situation. We had already declared bankruptcy, and yet our monthly expenses still exceeded our ability to pay. I had purchased a home after divorcing my first husband, and my new husband and I simply could not afford to pay the mortgage, owing to the fact that he was still paying child support to his two children from his first marriage. One day, while I was reeling from financial difficulty and so tired from always running on the hamster wheel without ever getting ahead, I angrily complained to God: "I'm just going to sell my house and buy a mobile home!" No sooner did those words come out of my mouth, than a warm feeling of peace come over my entire body. I knew in my heart that selling our home and purchasing a mobile home was the right thing to do.

So my husband and I began straightaway to ready our home for sale and to comb the market for a mobile home to move into. Many people thought I was CRAZY! My home was a beautiful 3 bedroom, 2 bath house that I had purchased while it was being built. When we shared our plans for what we were going to do, many people said that they could never live in a trailer, much less give up their home in order to do it. And, when we found our new home, we paid cash for our 1976 double wide with water damage, leaky plumbing, an insufficient air conditioning system and a rodent problem. Talk about taking a risk! Lucky for us, we did not know about the problems in the home until *after* we moved in. I say lucky because the risk involved in downsizing to a mobile home really scared me. Had I known the problems we would discover after we moved in, I would have been terrified, and maybe would not have moved!

But, here's what happened after we moved in. I began sleeping better. Our income exceeded our monthly expenses.

We began to dig ourselves out from debt. I began to have more emotional energy to devote to writing, and my creative energy began to flow. I finished my first book and began sending it off to publishers. I submitted my second book to Morgan James and obtained a publishing contract. Yes, I had sacrificed my home, but I fully believe that had we not taken that step, it might have been another six years before I finished the first book! And, once we were in the mobile home, our financial situation changed enough to allow us to devote financial resources toward launching my career as an author and professional speaker. For me, making the move to the 1976 Skyline represents the sacrifice that put me in a position to be able to take advantage of opportunity. Success, some have said, is the result of being prepared when opportunity arises. The move represented the sacrifice. The offer of the contract was the opportunity.

I provide these examples because I want to encourage you to look at your life and compare where you are today with where your dreams need to take you. Do you need to take a class to obtain the tools you need to get closer to what you dream of? Do you need to downsize your financial obligations? Do you need to get out and network with people? Only you can make an evaluation that helps you decide what risks and sacrifices you need to make. Ask yourself: "Is it worth it to sit still and do nothing? Am I willing to take the risks necessary to soar like an eagle, or am I a chicken?"

So, What Are You Going to Do About It?

I really believe that when you look at your dreams and compare where you want to be with where you are now, sacrifices and risks loom large. Perhaps that is the reason your dreams are still just dreams. What sacrifices do you need to make to position yourself so that you will be ready when opportunity knocks?

Your Assignment

Go back and get your work from the assignment at the end of Chapter One. Now look at it and listen to your inner voice that tells you what has to change in your life in order to make that dream a reality. Now, make a list of what has to happen. Carry that list around in your heart and think and pray and talk about what risks you need to take. Gather the strength you need to take the risks by becoming very familiar with your list. Work on getting ready to jump, knowing that the universe will meet you when you have the desire and are prepared!

CHAPTER 10

THE LEGACY OF A
BEAUTIFUL, STRONG,
COMPETENT, CAPABLE WOMAN

What Will You Leave To The Ones Who Follow You?

In my heart, I am a mother. I began training myself for the job as a small child. I believed my dolls were alive and that it was my job to nurture and care for them in the most gentle and genuine way. When I was 18, I went to Germany to be a nanny to four children in order to prove to myself that I could actually nurture real-live children. I was practicing for my most coveted role: motherhood. In my journals, which I began writing at a very young age, I often wrote to my future children: the things I wanted them to know, and my hopes for their happiness. I have placed quite a lot of thought into what the coming generation would need from me and how I could best provide that.

When I married my first husband, I expected to conceive a honeymoon baby and begin my career of motherhood. One year passed, and then two. Finally, it has been 18 years since my first dream of motherhood through the traditional methods. Unsuccessful fertility treatments and 18 years of marital relations have convinced me that biological motherhood simply isn't in the cards for me. But I do have two beautiful, strong adopted daughters. And, I try to give my best efforts to them.

As I am contemplating this last chapter of my book, I realize something else. I have the heart of a mother. It is from my mothering heart that the inspiration for this book sprang. I mother my daughters. I also mother the clients who come to my psychotherapy office. I have the desire to mother a world-wide community of women. I realize that my desires for my children who never materialized are the same as my desires for each of those I nurture today. What does it mean that I am a mother to so many? It means that I give my heart toward the fulfillment of a specific goal. Here is my goal: to provide the nurturing and support that develops the kind of independence where I am no longer needed. A few times, women clients of mine have left my psychotherapy office for the last time after 6 months or 4 years or 6 years of counseling. When they left my office for the last time, they were considerably different than they had been during our first meeting. Fear had been transformed into courage. Poor self-esteem had been changed into confidence and hope. Depression had turned to joy. Loneliness had given way to joyful relationships. The best part was that those changes permanently belonged to each of those women. And, as they left my office, they possessed the knowledge that continuous growth was part of their life pattern. They were happy, and they knew that no matter what their circumstances provided, the happiness was a permanent condition. What a gift it has been in my life to have been the vehicle for that type of metamorphosis! Because of it, I see so much beauty in every woman I meet – even before any changes have taken place.

Unfortunately, those experiences have also made me selfish. Selfish about the fact that I am no longer satisfied with helping one woman at a time, one hour at a time. Now, I wish to help so many more. That is why I wrote this book. I want to create an endless legacy of women who recognize their own value in the same way as the women who walked out of my office with such profound changes. I hope that my legacy is that of a beautiful, strong, competent, capable woman. I wish that in my path, I leave many such women who, in turn, leave similarly praiseworthy legacies. In a sense that emanates from deep within my soul, each woman who reads this book and dares to change her life is one of my daughters. Each woman who joins the world-wide community of support that we create is a sister, a friend. And I am also a daughter to women whose legacies of strength, hope and courage I hope to inherit.

It is true that no two of us are exactly the same. We each have different strengths and weaknesses. Let's grow together. Here is a child with an incredibly strong will – let us help her focus her will in a direction that brings her strength and success. When we do not get along, let us not call each other difficult, but "direct" or "goal-oriented," or similar adjectives that connote positive assumptions about each other. Let us value our direct sisters because we can trust them to tell us the truth – not to be rude, but to be honest. We have to remember, we are all in this together. How long have we tried to make it on our own and found ourselves needing and wanting more companionship, more support, more encouragement? All of those things are available to us if we will simply reach out an open hand toward one another.

Will you support me when I tell you what I need in order to nurture myself? I promise to tell you the truth rather than obey the rules that tell me I have to "be polite." Can we be honest with each other about what we need? Can we give each other permission to feed ourselves before the proverbial well runs dry?

Will you remind me to re-examine my priorities when you see that I've put myself on the back burner again? If you are my friend, my sister, my daughter, I will remind you. I promise. That is what this book and what www.GetOutoftheMud.com are all about. Being there for each other. It is imperative that we learn these principles so that we can teach them to our daughters. Let's give them permission from an early age to consider their own needs while making important decisions. If we do, I think they will experience less disappointment, fewer failed marriages, less burn-out, and more joyful lives. Let us teach our sons that women have needs, too. Let's teach our sons to be nurturing, caring men who take others' needs into consideration. We can do that by showing them that we value ourselves. Then, they will build relationships wherein their wives' happiness is as important as their own. And they will know how to support their companions in their efforts to live joyfully and effectively. We must live in a way that teaches the principles I've outlined in this book *by example* to our children.

As a mother and as a woman with multiple roles, it is easy to sometimes forget myself. It is not always easy to juggle all of my responsibilities. I know you share that experience with me. But I submit to you that when we allow our own needs to suffer, we also allow our family members to suffer. As young as seven years old, my rodeo bull-riding daughter could sense those times when I was neglecting myself. Although I never became a screaming maniac, she could see when I needed to re-align my priorities. She would ask me: "Mom, are you taking piano lessons any more? Are you getting massages?" The wisdom of a child is amazing. Let's preserve our daughter's wisdom by teaching them to *listen to themselves* because *we listen to ourselves* and teach them about that process.

As we do these things, we will experience an explosion of positive opportunities because our eyes will be open to what is good. We will give ourselves absolute permission to reach for what is good. Possibilities will develop. Passion will grow! Yes, we may need to choose among many good choices. We might have to let go of some choices in favor of others. Although I love to belly dance, my craving to dance has to be set aside for the time being in order to launch my book. Belly dance is a wonderful, inspiring, affirmative activity. But so is reaching out to women everywhere to inspire and affirm them. Don't you agree with me that the second choice is the better choice?

In every woman I see a vision of myself. And in every woman and child, we should see visions of each other. We should look for the good, the familiar, the qualities that we can embrace. We should build each other up until the undesirable qualities in each of us shrink because of neglect. We need to recognize those parts in each other that need recognition and validation and love. When we let go of that, we fight like cats. We lose our vision of the skies and what we can do when we strengthen one another.

Pull Yourself OUT of the MUD

Let's leave the fighting to our fur babies. Let's begin, today, to strengthen one another. I believe we owe that, at least *that*, to ourselves and to our children. Don't you?

So, What Are You Going To Do About It?

That's a really good question. What are you going to do?

CHAPTER NOTES

Chapter 2 Notes:

[1] *The New Lexicon Webster's Dictionary of the English Language*. Encyclopedic Edition. Lexicon Publications, Inc. 1987, New York.

[2] *The Dictionary of Family Psychology and Family Therapy*. Second Edition. Sauber, L'Abate, Weeks & Buchanan, Editors. SAGE publications , 1993.

[3] The height weight data for this chapter were collected from the following website: www.pbs.org.

[4] Ideal weight, for the purposes of this discussion, is derived from assuming that a woman 5 feet tall should weigh 100 pounds and that for every inch of height after 5 feet, 5 pounds should be added to the ideal. The healthy weight range is derived from allowing a ten percent deviation above and below the ideal weight.

[5] Source: www.news.bbc.co.uk

Chapter 3 Notes:

[1] "Muddy thinking patterns" are adaptations of Cognitive Distortions, identified by Aaron T. Beck in: *Cognitive Therapy of Depression.* Aaron T. Beck, A. John Rush, Brian F. Shaw, Gary Emery. The Guilford Press, 1979.

Chapter 7 Notes:

[1] Here I refer to the mother's face, because the mother is typically the most significant source of mirroring. However, this process can and does unfold with any significant caregiver from which a child develops her self-concept as she grows.

ABOUT THE AUTHOR

Tamara Johnson, M.S., LMFT, is a Licensed California Marriage and Family Therapist who specializes in empowering women to change personal and relationship patterns in significant ways that vastly improve their lives. As part of that work, she also focuses on strengthening the marriage relationships of the women who come to her private practice. She began her career as a therapist in 1997, when she graduated from Loma Linda University and worked for the next four years, training as a Marriage and Family Therapist Intern with The Family Connection and The Family Resource Center. Tamara opened The Center for Healthy Relationships in June, 2001.

During the process of her divorce in 2003, Tamara began exploring the patterns that had contributed to her having remained in a marriage 13 years in spite of indications that she should have left the marriage after the first month. Soon she discovered that similar patterns and habits of negative thinking and relating were evident in the lives of many women she encountered in her personal and professional life. In 2004, through a miraculous series of events, Tamara married her second husband, Michael Robert Johnson. Within the safety of her marriage to Michael, Tamara continued to explore old wounds and heal from past traumas. This book is the result of

Tamara's discoveries about herself during her first marriage and the process of healing that ensued with her second marriage. It is also the result of Tamara's witness that exploring the same principles with women in her private practice resulted in many women healing their own lives.

In addition to her Master's Degree in Marriage and Family Sciences from Loma Linda University, Tamara holds a Certificate in Family Life Education from the same institution. She graduated from the University of California at Riverside with a Bachelor's Degree in Psychology. She also holds an Associate of Science Degree in Mathematics and Natural Sciences from Riverside Community College.

Tamara is a member of Phi Beta Kappa and the California Association of Marriage and Family Therapists.

Tamara and Michael have been married four years and have a blended family of four children. Tamara and Michael live with Tamara's youngest child and their three cats in Southern California where Tamara stays busy writing, speaking professionally, providing trainings and workshops and maintaining her crusade to improve women's lives and relationships.

BONUS
Unlock the SECRETS
of Compatibility

Did you know that there is more to being compatible in your relationship than just matching your personalities to each other? Once you understand how your personality affects your compatibility, you are prepared to use that knowledge to improve your relationship! Without this knowledge, many couples believe their partner is behaving out of malicious motives rather than from differences in perspective.

As your free gift for purchasing Pull Yourself Out of the Mud, Tamara invites you to download your free mp3 recording: Unlock the SECRETS of Compatibility in Your Relationship. In this powerful, eye-opening session, Tamara will teach you how to understand yourself and your partner like never before. She will even teach you how to change your differences into qualities you appreciate in your partner!

DON'T WAIT!

Go to

www.GetOutoftheMud.com/Secrets

for your free mp3 download now!